New Braids and Designs
— IN —
MILANESE LACE

Patricia Read and Lucy Kincaid

New Braids and Designs
— IN —
MILANESE LACE

B.T. Batsford Ltd · London

First published 1994

Typeset by Servis Filmsetting Ltd, Manchester
and printed in Great Britain by
Bath Press, Bath

Published by
B T Batsford Ltd
9 Blenheim Court
Brewery Road
London N7 9NT

A member of the Chrysalis Group plc

A catalogue record for this book is available from
the British Library

ISBN 0 7134 8678 3

Acknowledgements

We would like to thank all those who have
encouraged us to produce *New Braids and
Designs in Milanese Lace* and who have
made lace for the book. Our special thanks
go to John Read, who has produced such
beautiful photographs. We are also grateful
to Aurora Art Publications, and to the
Dover Pictorial Archive Series.

Frontispiece: Serpents. Designed by
Jane Read and worked by
Marjorie Ross (see p. 83)

Contents

Introduction

Milanese has a greater variety of decorative stitches within the braid than any other lace. It is this variety, added to the baroque style of its designs, that makes Milanese the most beautiful of Italian laces. Gold and silver threads were used in the earliest examples, and because of this very little has survived; the lace would have been melted down for the value of its metal. But what little there is shows us that, though decorative, the early work had none of the intricate braids we associate with later Milanese made with linen thread. It can be reasonably assumed that workers then, as today, found flax more pliable than metallic threads, since it allowed them to make fancy stitches without breaking the thread. Nowadays, those who make this lace have a wealth of ideas to explore and develop. In our first book, *Milanese Lace*, we detailed thirty braids. In this book there are a further forty-one.

Milanese lace developed throughout the seventeenth century and, in the best tradition of Italian art, the designs were easy-flowing curves and elegant scrolls in floral and leaf forms. However, the beauty of the lace was not due only to the design, but also to the decoration within the braid work. Milanese lace is made in sections called free or part lace, which are then put together to produce a flounce (see p. 92). The flounce can be of any length, according to requirements. To make the individual sections or motifs, the braid is turned repeatedly, building up a shape such as a flower or leaf. Four, five or more braids will be put together and joined with pillow sew-

ings, and there will be only one place where the bobbins begin and another where they are sewn off. To some present-day lacemakers the advantage of this method is obvious: relatively few bobbins are used on the pillow, usually between twelve and twenty pairs. For others, however, there is a major disadvantage: the sewings, which require a skill and speed that come only with practice. In the earlier part of the seventeenth century, these sewings would also be used to join the motifs themselves in order to assemble a flounce. The motifs were mostly arranged without connecting bars or surrounding net, and an excellent example of this style can be seen in a panel (ref. no. 42–1903) in the lace collection of the Victoria and Albert Museum, London. Modern interpretations of this style are shown on pp. 81 and 90 of *Milanese Lace* and in the Basket, Finial and Collar patterns (pp. 56, 88 and 106) in this book.

Later in the seventeenth century the motifs became more spaced out and were joined with connecting bars composed of twisted threads, plaits or false plaits. The plaits themselves often had picots in a decorative form (see, for example, the Milanese mat in *The Art of Bobbin Lace* by L.A. Tebbs,* or the modern version on p. 117 of *Milanese Lace*. Such plaits and picots were the main feature of Venetian bobbin lace, a straight lace made in Italy from an early date, examples of which can be found in a facsimile edition of a pattern book first published in 1559 called *Le Pompe*.† Narrow bands of this work were used to trim the edges of Milanese flounces. By the end of the seventeenth century and the beginning of the eighteenth, the spaces between the motifs of the flounces were filled with net work, a Valenciennes-type ground which would be added after the motifs had been assembled.

Milanese lace was usually made for church vestments and altar cloths. The two spiral braids shown in this book, Ammonite and Chevron (pp. 41 and 42), have in fact been taken from an alb in the collection of Mrs Doreen Wright. The lace was also made for the nobility, who would have designs worked to include coats of arms or to commemorate special events. In addition, many pieces depicted classical or Biblical scenes; the figure work we like to do today is by no means a modern idea! What has changed, however, is the use to which we now put our lace. It is good to learn from the work that has been done in the past, but for lace to be a living craft it should not stand still. We need to build on what we know, develop the techniques and make them our own. We can preserve the traditions, which for many give

the greatest pleasure, but we can also experiment and perhaps surprise ourselves with our own achievements. The work in this book comes under both categories: traditional and modern. It will be seen that even in the coloured lace it has been possible to retain the traditional character of Milanese, whilst in the Shepherdess design (p. 69) there is a very different, even controversial, technique to consider.

We hope that the work in this book will inspire you not just to make some of the patterns, but to create your own designs. To a great extent, the fascination of lacemaking for the worker lies in the pleasure of hands on bobbins. But we need to look ahead. Let us take the lace of the seventeenth century into the twenty-first by putting our own stamp on it.

Patricia Read and Lucy Kincaid
September 1993

*Originally published 1907, reprinted by Paul Minet, 1972.
†Reprinted by Ruth Bean (eds Levey and Payne), 1983.

Starting Braid Work

The decorated braids on pp. 1–42 are listed in alphabetical order. If you have not previously attempted this particular form of braid work, try working a few samples before starting a pattern. Make the samples about 8 cm. long and they will also be useful for reference when choosing braids for other patterns. Note that some braids are more open, while others have a very closely worked texture.

Study the following abbreviations before starting.

cls	cloth (or whole) stitch
edge st	Cloth stitch worker with edge pair, twist both pairs twice. Pin inside both pairs.
hs	half stitch
lt	left
pr prs	pair, pairs
rep	repeat
rt	right
st	stitch
thro	through
ts	turning stitch*
tw	twist
w ws	worker, workers (or weaver/s)
x t	cross – turn (half stitch)
x t x	cross – turn – cross (cloth stitch)
x t t	cross – turn – turn, etc.

* Turning stitch has been indicated on the diagrams by a circle (○).

Turning Stitch

This is often used when the pattern requires holes to be made, and when a worker has to turn in the work but has no pinhole to support it. It is also used to divide a braid, thus giving two worker pairs.

There are several ways of making a turning stitch. Throughout this book the following method has been used:

cross – turn – cross – turn – cross

i.e. work two half stitches then cross the two centre bobbins left over right. (Think of the five movements as the five fingers on one hand.)

It will be seen from the diagram above that one thread from each pair changes place and becomes part of the opposite pair. However, alternative methods may be used if found to be satisfactory.

CHAPTER ONE

The Braids

Bubbles

14 prs

Work in cls throughout.

Work ts with W and centre pr. Both these prs are now Ws. Work lt W to lt thro 2 prs, tw W twice, thro 1 pr, tw W once, thro 2 prs, tw W twice, edge st and pin. Leave. Work rt W to the rt in similar manner. Leave.

* Centre 4 prs:
 Ts with 2 lt prs.
 Ts with 2 rt prs.
 Using each pr as 1 thread, work 1 cls.
 Using threads singly: ts with 2 lt prs and ts with 2 rt prs. These are called the *plait prs.*

Lt W thro 2 prs, tw W once, thro next pr, tw W twice, then 1 cls thro the 2 plait prs using each of these 2 prs as 1 thread, tw W 3 times.

Rt W thro to lt in a similar manner.

Work cls with the 2 Ws, tw both these prs 3 times. The Ws have now changed sides.

Work ts with each set of plait prs.

Work lt W thro the 2 plait prs using each of these 2 prs as 1 thread, tw W twice, thro next pr, tw W once, thro 2 prs, tw W twice, edge st and pin. Leave.

Work rt W to rt in similar manner.*

Rep from * to * for desired length.

To finish: work ts with Ws in the centre.

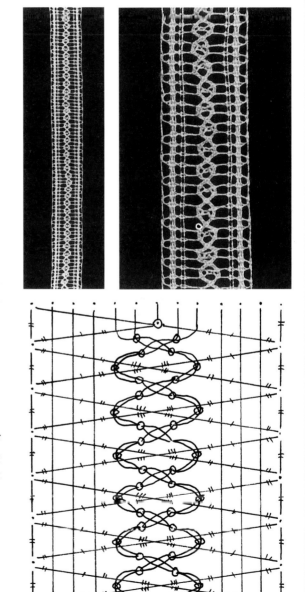

Chicane

16 prs

Work in cls throughout.

Work ts with W and centre pr. Both these prs are now Ws. Work lt W to the lt thro 6 prs, tw twice, edge st and pin. Work rt W to the rt in similar manner.

Work rt W thro 5 prs to lt, ts with next pr, return with the rt pr thro 5 prs to the rt, tw W twice, edge st and pin. Leave.

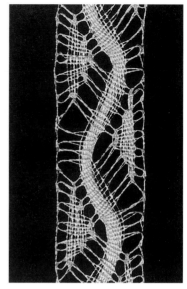

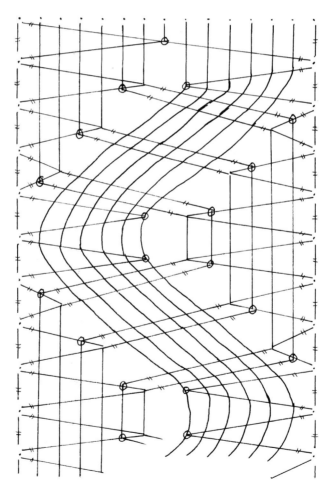

Left side:

Work W thro 6 prs to rt, leave the W and work ts with the last pr passed thro and the next pr to the lt, work the lt of these 2 prs thro 4 prs to lt, tw W twice, edge st and pin.

Work W thro 4 prs to rt, leave the W and work ts with the last pr passed thro and the next pr to the lt, work the lt of these 2 prs thro 2 prs to lt, tw W twice, edge st and pin.

Work W thro 2 prs to rt, leave the W and work ts with the last pr passed thro and the next pr to the lt. Tw twice the lt of these 2 prs, edge st and pin. Leave the W and edge pr.

Tw twice the next 6 prs and work each of them in turn thro the 6 passive prs on the rt side. Tw twice the 6 prs that are now on the rt.

(Work the lt W thro the 5 passive prs and make a ts with the 6th pr. Return with the lt pr to the lt edge, tw W twice, edge st and pin.) Rep once more.

* Right side:

Work ts with W and next pr to lt, work thro 1 more pr.

Return with last pr passed thro to rt edge, tw twice, edge st and pin.

Work W thro 2 prs, ts with next pr, thro 1 more pr.

Return with last pr passed thro to rt edge, tw twice, edge st and pin.

Work thro 4 prs, ts with next pr, thro 1 more pr.

Return with last pr passed thro to rt edge, tw twice, edge st and pin.

Work W thro 6 prs, leave W and work ts with the last pr passed thro and the next pr to the rt.

Work the rt of these 2 prs thro 4 prs to rt, tw W twice, edge st and pin.

Work W thro 4 prs, leave W and work ts with the last pr passed thro and the next pr to the rt.

Work the rt of these 2 prs thro 2 prs to the rt, tw W twice, edge st and pin.

Work W thro 2 prs, leave W and work ts with the last pr passed thro and the next pr to the rt, tw twice, edge st and pin. Leave W and edge pr.

Tw twice the next 6 prs and work each of them in turn thro the 6 passive prs on the lt side. Tw twice the 6 prs that are now on the lt.

(Work the rt W thro the 5 passive prs and make a ts with the 6th pr. Return with the rt pr to the rt edge, tw twice, edge st and pin.) Rep once more.

Left side:

Work in similar manner to right side.*

Rep from * to * for desired length.

Cross-bud

16 prs

Work in cls braid.

The divisions (which are optional) are made by twisting each passive pr 3 times.

Work 5 rows of cls.

In next row work ts with W and centre pr. Both these prs are now Ws.

Left side:

Lt W thro 6 prs to lt, tw W twice, edge st and pin. W thro 6 prs to centre, leave the W. Make a ts with the last pr passed thro and next pr to lt. Lt of these 2 prs is new W, work it thro 4 prs to lt, tw W twice, edge st and pin.

W thro 3 prs to rt, ts with next pr. Lt of these 2 prs is new W, work it thro 3 prs to lt, tw W twice, edge st and pin. Leave.

Right side:

Work in similar manner to lt side.

Centre 4 prs:

Tw each pr twice.
Work 2 lt prs thro 2 rt prs in cls.
Tw each pr twice.

Left side:

W thro 4 prs, ts with next pr and cls thro next pr. Last pr passed thro is new W, return thro 5 prs, tw W twice, edge st and pin. Leave.

Right side:

Work in same way as lt side.
Work both Ws to centre and make a ts. One pr remains as a passive and the other is the W.

Continue in cls braid, working at least 5 rows before making divisions or another cross-bud.

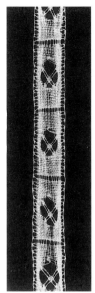
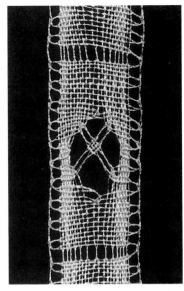

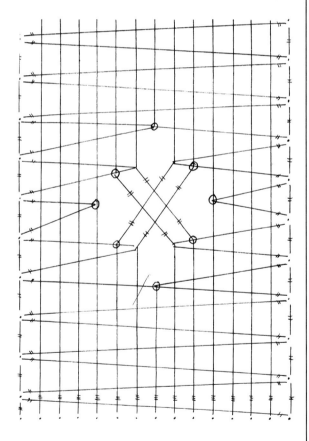

Cross-net

14 prs

Work ts with W and centre pr. Both these prs are now Ws. Work the lt W to the lt in cls thro 5 prs, tw twice, edge st and pin, and work the rt W to the rt in a similar manner. Leave. With the 2 centre passive prs work (cls and tw) twice (small plait made).

*Left side:
   Work W thro 3 prs in cls, ts with next pr, tw rt pr once, and return with lt pr thro 3 prs, tw twice, edge st and pin. W thro 3 prs in cls, tw W once.

Right side:
   Work in similar manner to lt side.

Cross-net:
   This is made with the centre 6 prs, each twisted once. Work cls and tw once throughout:
   Lt centre pr thro 2 prs to lt.
   Rt centre pr thro 2 prs to rt.
   Lt centre pr thro 2 prs to rt.
   Lt centre pr thro 1 pr to lt.
   Two centre prs.
   Outside lt pr thro 2 prs to rt.
   Outside rt pr thro 2 prs to lt.
   Two centre prs (cls and tw) twice.
   Lt pr thro 3 prs to lt tw W twice, edge st and pin.
   Rt pr thro 3 prs to rt tw W twice, edge st and pin.*

   Rep from * to * for desired length, finishing with a cross-net.

Note Pull up the cross-net carefully. If it bunches too tightly ease it out with a needle pin. Try to keep the cross-nets in line down the centre of the braid.

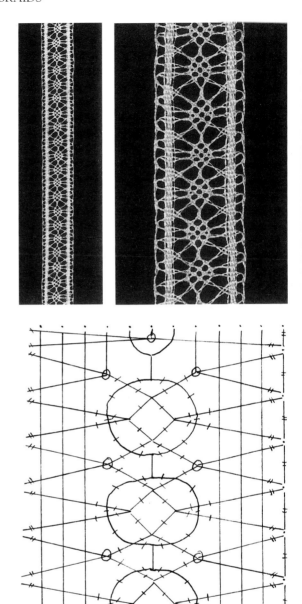

Daisy 1

16 prs

Work in cls throughout.

Work ts with W and centre pr. Both these prs are now Ws. Work lt W to lt thro 6 prs, tw W twice, edge st and pin. Leave. Work rt W to rt in similar manner. Leave.

* Centre 4 prs:
    Work 2 lt prs thro 2 rt prs, then tw all 4 prs twice.

Left side:
    W thro 4 prs, ts with next pr, cls thro next pr, return with lt pr thro 5 prs, tw W twice, edge st and pin. W thro 6 prs. Leave.

Right side:
    Work in similar manner to lt side.

The 2 Ws are now in the centre. Tw each pr once, work cls and tw. Ws have now changed sides.

Left side:
    Work lt W thro 6 prs to lt, tw twice, edge st and pin. W thro 6 prs, return with lt pr and make a ts with next pr, lt pr thro 4 prs, tw twice, edge st and pin. W thro 4 prs, tw twice. Leave.

Right side:
    Work in similar manner to lt side.

Centre 4 prs:
    Tw each pr twice. Work lt 2 prs thro rt 2 prs.
    Lt W thro 2 prs to rt.
    Rt W thro 2 prs to lt.
    Cls with 2 Ws. Ws have changed sides.
    Lt W thro 2 prs to lt, tw W twice, thro 4 prs, tw W twice, edge st and pin.
    Work rt W to rt in similar manner.*

Rep from * to * for desired length. Finish with the centre crossing of 4 prs.

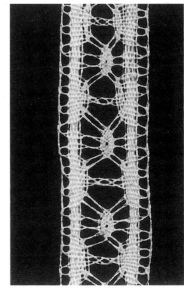

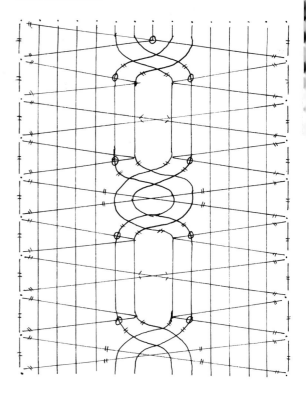

Daisy 2

16 prs

Work in cls throughout.

Work ts with W and centre pr. Both these prs are now Ws. Work lt W to lt thro 6 prs, tw W twice, edge st and pin. Leave. Work rt W to rt in similar manner. Leave.

* Centre 4 prs:
    Work lt 2 prs thro rt 2 prs, then tw all 4 prs twice.

Left side:
    W thro 4 prs, ts with next pr, cls thro next pr, return with lt pr thro 5 prs, tw W twice, edge st and pin.
    W thro 6 prs, return with lt pr, ts with next pr, lt of these 2 prs thro 4 prs, tw W twice, edge st and pin. Leave.

Right side:
    Work in similar manner to lt side.

Centre 4 prs:
    Tw each pr twice. Work lt 2 prs thro rt 2 prs.

Left side:
    W thro 4 prs, tw W twice, thro 1 pr, ts with next pr. Return with lt pr thro 1 pr, tw W twice, thro 4 prs, tw W twice, edge st and pin. Leave.

Right side:
    Work in similar manner to lt side.*

Rep from * to * for desired length. Finish with the centre crossing of 4 prs.

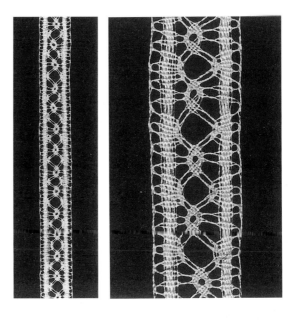

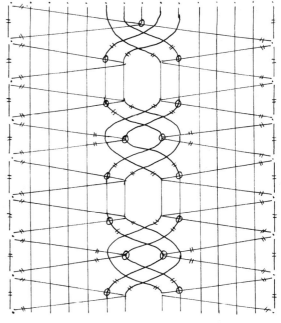

Dewdrops

15 prs

Leave edge pr and W on lt. Tw each of the 12 passive prs once.

* Divide the passive prs into 4 sets of 3 prs. Work each set thus:

Work lt pr thro the 2 prs to the rt in cls and tw.

[†] (Work W thro each of the 12 passive prs in cls and tw, tw W once more, edge st and pin.) Rep this row once more.[†]

Leave edge pr and W on lt. Divide the passives into 4 sets of 3 prs. Work each set thus:

Work rt pr thro the 2 prs to the lt in cls and tw.

Rep from[†] to [†]*.

Rep from * to * for desired length.

Variation

The outside sets of 3 prs on the lt and rt may be worked as straight passives in cls, leaving 2 sets of dewdrops in the centre.

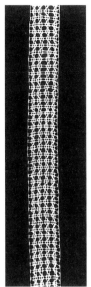
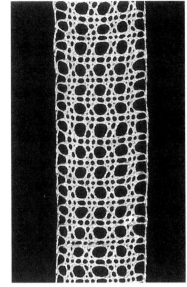

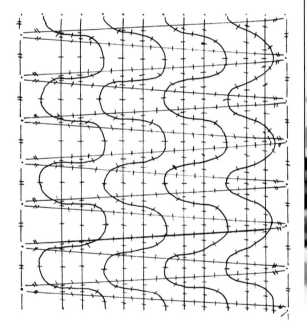

Fish 1

13 prs

** Leave edge pr and W on lt. Tw first passive pr once. (Next 2 prs cls and tw) rep 3 more times. Tw next pr once.

* Work W thro every pr in cls and tw, tw W once more, edge st and pin. Leave.*

(Next 2 prs cls) rep 4 more times.

† Work W (thro 2 prs in cls, tw W once) rep 4 more times, tw W once more, edge st and pin. †

(Work W thro every pr in cls, tw W twice, edge st and pin.) Rep this row once more. Then rep the row marked † to †. Leave.

(Next 2 prs cls and tw.) Rep 4 more times. Then rep the row marked * to *.

Tw next pr once (next 2 prs cls) rep 3 more times, tw next pr once.

‡ Work W thro 1 pr, tw W once (thro next 2 prs, tw W once) rep 3 more times, thro next pr, tw W twice, edge st and pin. ‡

(Work W thro every pr in cls, tw W twice, edge st and pin.) Rep this row once more.

Then rep the row marked ‡ to ‡. Leave.

Rep from ** for desired length.

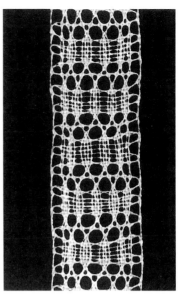

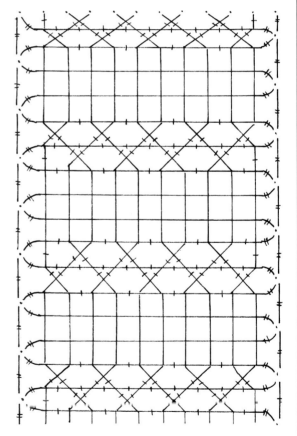

Fish 2

13 prs

Leave edge pr and W on lt. Divide the 10 passive prs into 5 sets of 2 prs and work 1 cls with each set.

† * (Work W thro 2 prs in cls, tw W twice) 5 times, edge st and pin.*

Rep from * to * once more.

Divide passives into 5 sets of 2 prs and work cls and tw with each set.

Divide the centre 8 passives into 4 sets of 2 prs and work cls with each set.

Work W in cls thro 1 pr, tw W once (W thro 2 prs, tw W once) 4 times, W thro 1 pr, tw W twice, edge st and pin.

** Work W in cls thro 10 passives, tw W twice, edge st and pin.**

Rep from ** to ** once more.

Work W in cls thro 1 pr, tw W once (W thro 2 prs, tw W once) 4 times, W thro 1 pr, tw W twice, edge st and pin.

Divide centre 8 passives into 4 sets of 2 prs and work cls with each set.

Tw once the 10 passive prs and divide them into 5 sets of 2 prs and work cls with each set. †

Rep from † to † for desired length.

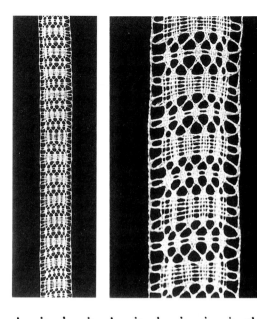

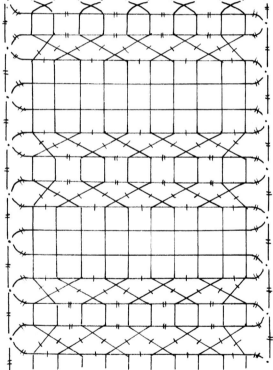

Fish 3

16 prs

Work in cls throughout. Work W from lt to rt thro 3 prs, tw W twice, thro 4 prs, tw W twice, thro 4 more prs, tw W twice, thro 2 prs, tw W twice, edge st and pin. Return thro 2 prs. Leave.

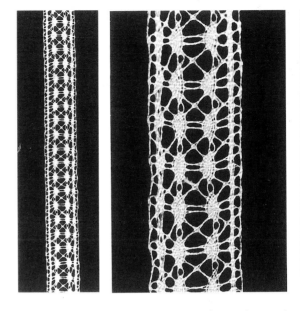

* From the lt:

Work 2nd passive pr thro 3rd passive pr. Leave.

Work 4th and 5th passive prs thro 6th and 7th prs. Leave.

Work 8th and 9th passive prs thro 10th and 11th prs. Leave.

Centre 10 prs:

Tw each pr twice.

Lt 2 prs cls and tw twice.

Next 2 prs, pin between (make pin-holes as required).

Next 2 prs, cls and tw twice.

Next 2 prs pin between.

Next 2 prs cls and tw twice.

Centre 8 prs:

Lt 2 prs thro 2 prs to rt. Leave.

Next 2 prs thro 2 prs to rt. Leave.

Work 3rd passive pr from lt thro 2 prs to lt, tw W twice, edge st and pin. Return thro 1 pr only and leave.

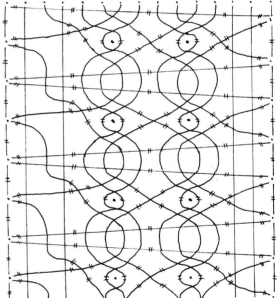

Work 3rd passive pr from rt thro 2 prs to rt, tw W twice, edge st and pin. Return thro 2 prs, tw W twice, thro 4 prs, tw W twice, thro 4 prs, tw W twice, thro 3 prs, tw W twice, edge st and pin. Return thro 3 prs, tw W twice, thro 4 prs, tw W twice, thro 4 prs, tw W twice, thro 2 prs, tw W twice, edge st and pin. Return thro 2 prs. Leave.*

Rep from * to * for desired length.

Grenades

15prs

Work 2 rows of cls with edge st.

* Divide the 12 passive prs into 3 sets of 4 prs.
Work each set as follows:
   Cls with lt 2 prs.
   Cls with rt 2 prs.
   Using each pr as one thread work cls with
the 4 prs.
   Using the threads singly again:
   Cls with lt 2 prs.
   Cls with rt 2 prs.

When each of the 3 sets has been worked in
this way, continue as follows:
   (Work W thro each passive pr in cls and tw
once, extra tw before edge st and pin) rep this
row 3 more times but in the last row do not
twist the passive prs.*

Rep from * to * for desired length, finishing
with the crossing of each set.

Note If prefered, 1 grenade may be worked
in the centre, the passive prs on each side
being worked in cls.

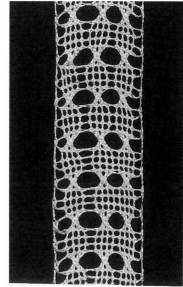

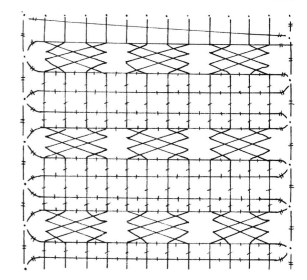

Hooked 1

12 prs

No W required (leave as a passive).

Centre 8 prs:
Tw each pr twice and divide into 2 sets of 4 prs. Work each set as follows:
2 centre prs cls and tw twice.
2 lt prs cls and tw twice.
2 rt prs cls and tw twice.
2 centre prs cls and tw twice.

* Left side:
Work 3rd pr from lt to the lt thro 1 pr, cls and tw W twice and passive once, edge st and pin. (Return thro inner edge pr and next pr, cls and tw. Return to lt with last pr passed thro and work cls and tw thro 1 pr, tw W once more, edge st and pin) rep twice more. Return thro inner edge pr, cls and tw, W once more.

Right side:
Work in similar manner to lt side.

Centre spider:
Using centre 4 prs work as follows:
2 centre prs cls and tw twice.
2 lt prs cls and tw twice.
2 rt prs cls and tw twice.
2 centre prs cls and tw twice.
2 lt prs cls and tw twice.
2 rt prs cls and tw twice.
2 centre prs cls and tw twice.

Left spider:
With the 2 lt prs from centre spider and the next 2 prs to the lt work another spider.

Right spider:
With the 2 rt prs from the centre spider and the next 2 prs to the rt, work another spider.*

Rep from * to * for desired length, finishing with half-made lt and rt spiders.

Note A variation on this design may be made giving only one twist instead of two on all the crossings. This would be suitable for a narrower braid.

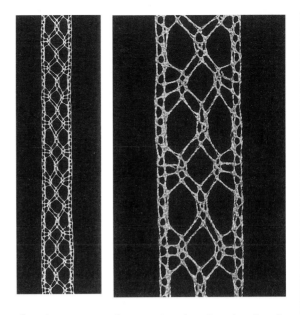

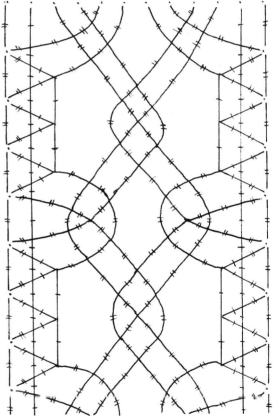

Hooked 2

12 prs

Work in cls and tw twice throughout. W left as a passive.

Centre 8 prs:
  Divide into 2 sets of 4 prs.
  Work each set: lt 2 prs thro rt 2 prs.

* Spider with centre 4 prs:
  Lt 2 prs thro rt 2 prs.
  Work 2 lt prs.
  Work 2 rt prs.
  Work 2 centre prs.

Left side:
  3rd pr from lt thro 2 prs to lt. Pin under 2 prs and close pin with 2 inside prs.
  4th pr from lt thro 3 prs to lt. Pin under 2 prs and close pin with 2 inside prs.
  Work lt spider with 3rd, 4th, 5th and 6th prs from lt.

Right side:
  Work in similar manner to lt side.*

Rep from * to * for desired length.

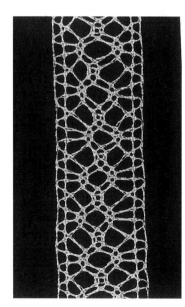

Italian Spider

15 prs

W on rt of braid.

Work W in cls thro 7 passive prs and ts with next pr. Both these prs are now Ws. Both prs work out to each edge: the lt W to the lt and the rt W to the rt. At each edge, pin under 2 prs and close pin with inside pr in cls and tw. Leave.

Centre 9 passive prs:
  Work each of the 3 lt prs in turn thro the rt 6 prs in cls.
  Tw once the lt 3 prs and the rt 3 prs.
  Tw 3 times the centre 3 prs.

Set aside the 9 prs on rt.

Net ground: Work in cls and tw with the lt 6 prs.
  Work the 3rd pr from lt thro 3 prs to rt.
  Work the (new) 3rd pr from lt to the lt thro 2 edge prs, pin, close the pin with the inner edge pr and work thro 2 more prs to the rt.

Work the (new) 3rd pr from lt to the lt, thro 2 edge prs, pin, close the pin with the inner edge pr and work thro 1 more pr to the rt.

Work the (new) 3rd pr from lt to the lt, thro 2 edge prs, pin, close the pin with the inner edge pr.

Set aside these 6 prs and the 3 centre prs (which are twisted 3 times). Work the net ground with the rt 6 prs in similar manner to lt side.

Work lt spider in cls:

Prs 4, 5 and 6 from lt work thro the centre 3 prs.

Intersect the spider by working the 3rd pr from lt edge thro all these 6 prs, tw once, cls and tw thro the next pr to the rt. The lt of these two returns to lt thro the 6 prs, tw once, cls and tw thro the 2 edge prs, pin and close the pin. Leave.

Complete the spider by working the 3 lt prs thro the 3 rt prs, tw lt 3 prs once and rt 3 prs three times.

Work the 6th pr from rt, which intersected the spider, in cls and tw thro 4 prs to rt, edge st and pin, close pin. Leave.

Work the net ground on the lt with the lt 6 prs. Work spider on rt in similar manner to lt spider, using centre 3 prs which have been twisted 3 times and 3 prs to the rt. Work the net ground on the rt with the rt 6 prs.

Continue in this manner so that the order of working is:

Spider on lt

Net ground on lt

Spider on rt

Net ground on rt

Finish with spider on rt and net ground on both sides, then work 3 lt passive prs thro 6 prs on rt. Work Ws from both sides to centre and make a ts, 1 pr remaining as W and 1 pr becoming a passive.

Turn diagram upside down to see the method of finishing.

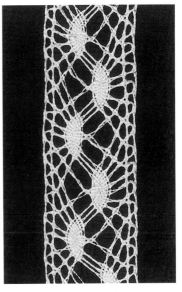
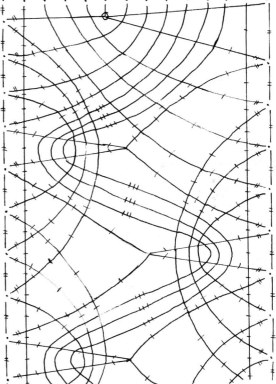

Lattice 1

13 prs

* Leave edge pr and W on lt.

(Take next 2 passive prs and work cls. Leave) 5 times. Leave the rt edge pr unworked.

† (Work W thro 2 prs in cls, tw W once) 5 times, tw W once more, edge st and pin.†

Rep from † to † once more.

** Work W thro 1 pr in cls, tw W once. (W thro 2 prs, tw W once) 4 times, W thro 1 pr, tw W twice, edge st and pin.**

Rep from ** to ** once more.

Leave edge pr and W on lt. Tw once 1st passive pr (take next 2 passive prs and work cls) 4 times, tw once last passive pr.

Rep from ** to ** twice.

Rep from † to † twice.*

Rep from * to * for desired length, finishing with the crossing of the passive prs.

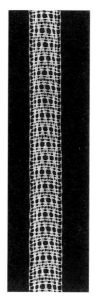
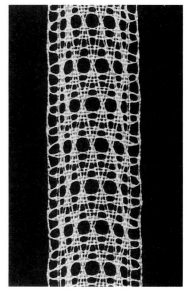

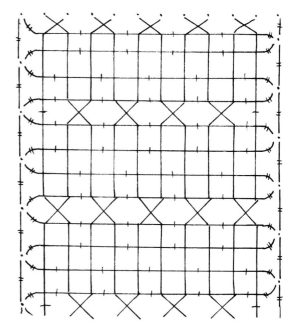

Lattice 2

15 prs

* Leave edge pr and W on lt. Divide centre 8 passive prs into 2 sets of 4 prs. With each set work a 4-pr crossing thus:

　Use 2 bobbins as 1 thread work 1 cls.

† Work W in cls thro 2 prs, tw W twice. (W thro 4 prs, tw W twice) 2 times, W thro 2 prs, tw W twice, edge st and pin.†

Rep from † to † twice more.

** (Work W in cls thro 4 prs, tw W twice) 3 times.**

Rep from ** to ** twice more.
Leave edge pr and W on lt. Divide passive prs into 3 sets of 4 prs. With each set work a 4-pr crossing (as above).

Rep from ** to ** 3 times.

Rep from † to † 3 times.*

Rep from * to * for desired length, finishing with sets of 4-pr crossings.

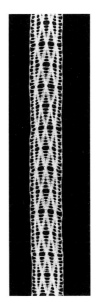
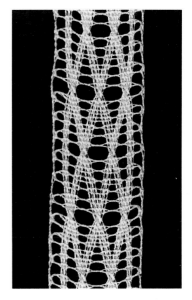

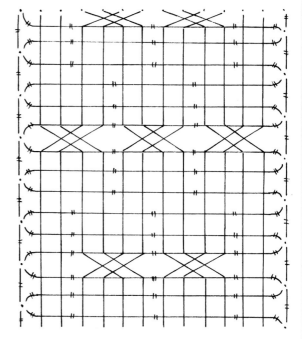

Lattice 3

15 prs

* Leave edge pr and W on lt. Divide the 12 passive prs into 3 sets of 4 prs. With each set work a 4-pr crossing thus:

Use 2 bobbins as 1 thread and work 1 cls.

† (Work W in cls thro 2 prs, tw W twice) rep 5 more times, edge st and pin.†

Rep from † to † once more.

Leave edge pr and W.

Work cls with first 2 passive prs. Divide next 8 passive prs into 2 sets of 4 prs and work a 4-pr crossing with each set, as above. Work cls with last 2 passive prs.

** (Work W in cls thro 2 prs, tw W twice) rep 5 more times, edge st and pin.**

Rep from ** to ** once more.*

Rep from * to * for desired length, finishing with a 4-pr crossing.

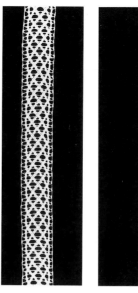

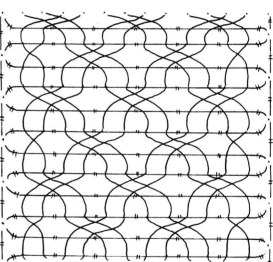

Lotus 1

15 prs

* Leave edge pr and W on lt. Work first 2 passive prs in cls. Leave. Divide the next 8 prs into 2 sets of 4 prs and work a 4-pr crossing with each set thus:

Using 2 bobbins as 1 thread, work 1 cls.

Then using the bobbins singly, work 1 cls with 2 lt prs and 1 cls with 2 rt prs.

Work last 2 passive prs in cls. Leave. Divide all the passives into 3 sets of 4 prs and with each set work a 4-pr crossing thus:

Using 2 bobbins as 1 thread, work 1 cls.

† (Work W in cls thro 4 prs, tw W twice) rep twice more, edge st and pin.† Rep from † to † twice more.

** Work W in cls thro 2 prs, tw W twice, W thro 4 prs, tw W twice, W thro 4 more prs, tw W twice, W thro 2 prs, tw W twice, edge st and pin.**

Rep from ** to ** twice more.*

Rep from * to * for desired length, finishing with the 4-pr crossings.

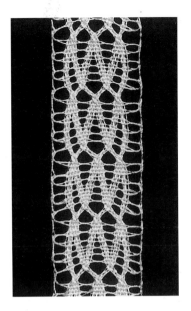
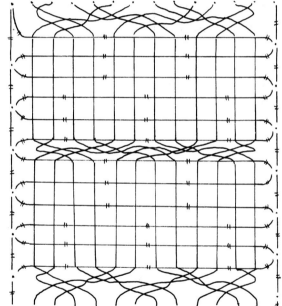

Lotus 2

15 prs

* Leave edge pr and W on lt. Divide the centre 8 passives prs into 2 sets of 4 prs. With each of these 2 sets work a 4-pr crossing thus:

Using 2 bobbins as 1 thread work 1 cls.

† (Work W thro 4 prs in cls, tw W twice) 3 times, edge st and pin.†

Rep from † to † twice more.

** Work W thro 2 prs in cls, tw W twice (work W thro 4 prs in cls, tw W twice) rep once more, W thro 2 prs, tw W twice, edge st and pin.**

Rep from ** to ** twice more.

Leave edge pr and W. Divide passive prs into 3 sets of 4 prs. With each of these 3 sets work a 4-pr crossing thus:

Using 2 bobbins as 1 thread work 1 cls.

Rep from ** to ** 3 times.

Rep from † to † 3 times.*

Rep from * to * for desired length, finishing with a 4-pr crossing.

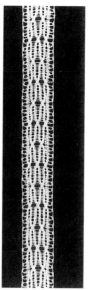
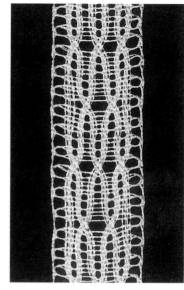

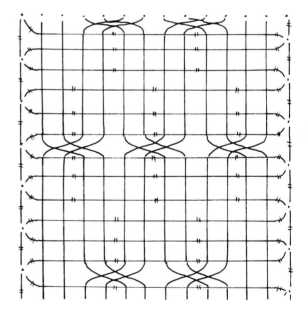

Lotus 3

15 prs

Work 2 rows of cls with edge st.

* Leave edge pr and W on lt. Divide passive prs into 3 sets of 4 prs. With each set work a 4-pr crossing thus:

    Using 2 bobbins as 1 thread work 1 cls.

† Work W thro 2 prs in cls, tw W once, repeat to end of row, tw W once more, edge st and pin.†

Rep from † to † 5 more times*

Rep from * to * for desired length.

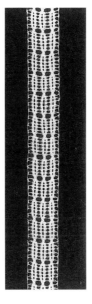
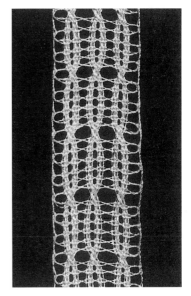

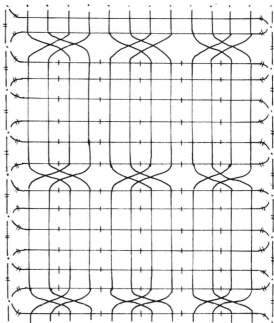

Meander with Ground

14 prs

Work W from lt thro 2 prs in cls and tw, then 4 prs in cls. Work ts with W and next pr. Both these prs are now Ws and work out to each edge: the lt W thro 4 prs to lt, tw W once, cls and tw thro 2 prs, tw W once more, edge st and pin under 2 prs, and the rt W thro 2 prs to rt, tw W once, cls and tw thro 2 prs, tw W once more, edge st and pin. Leave.

Work 4th passive pr from lt thro 4 prs to rt in cls, tw once. Leave.

Work 3rd passive pr from lt thro same 4 prs to rt in cls, tw once. Leave.

Left side:
   * Work W thro 2 prs in cls and tw, thro 3 prs in cls and ts with next pr.
   Return with lt pr thro 3 prs in cls, tw W once, thro 2 prs in cls and tw, tw W once more, edge st and pin.*
   Rep from * to * once more. Leave.

† Right side:
   Work W thro 4 prs in cls and tw, thro next 4 prs in cls, tw W once. Leave.
   Take 4th pr from rt as new W and work to rt thro 2 prs in cls and tw, tw W once more, edge st and pin.
   Return thro 3 prs in cls and tw, thro next 4 prs in cls, tw W once. Leave.
   Take 4th pr from rt as new W and work to rt thro 2 prs in cls and tw, tw W once more, edge st and pin.
   ** W thro 2 prs to lt in cls and tw, thro 3 prs in cls, ts with next pr. Return with the rt of these 2 prs, cls thro 3 prs, tw W once, thro next 2 prs in cls and tw, tw W once more, edge st and pin.**
   Rep from ** to ** once more.

Left side:
   Work in similar manner to rt side.†

Rep from † to † for desired length.

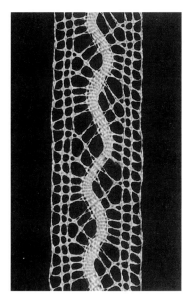
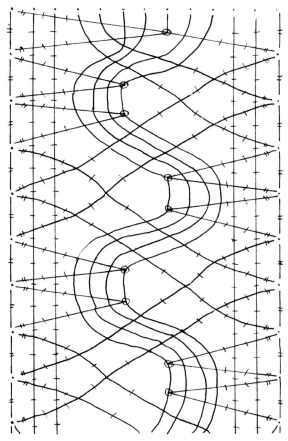

Meander with Rose

18 prs

Work in cls throughout.

Work ts with W and centre pr. Both these prs are now Ws. Work the lt W to the lt thro 7 prs, tw W twice, edge st and pin. Work rt W to rt in similar manner. Leave

Work 5th passive pr from rt thro 6 prs to lt. Leave.

Work 4th passive pr from rt thro 6 prs to lt. Leave.

Rt W thro 3 prs to lt, return to rt with last pr passed thro, tw W twice, edge st and pin.

(Rt W thro 3 prs to lt, tw W once, thro 5 more prs, ts with next pr, return thro 5 prs, tw W once, thro 3 more prs, tw W twice, edge st and pin.) Rep twice more. Leave.

* Left side:
    W thro 3 prs, return to lt with last pr passed thro, tw W twice, edge st and pin.
    W thro 1 pr, tw lt pr twice, edge st and pin. Leave.

Rose crossing with the 2nd, 3rd, 4th and 5th passive prs from lt:
    Tw each pr once.
    2 lt prs cls and tw.
    2 rt prs cls and tw.
    2 centre prs cls and tw.
    2 lt prs cls and tw.
    2 rt prs cls and tw.
    2 centre prs cls and tw.
    2 lt prs cls and tw.
    2 rt prs cls and tw.
    Work the 2 rt prs thro 6 prs to the rt. Leave.

Lt W thro 3 prs, return with last pr passed thro, tw W twice, edge st and pin.

(W thro 3 prs, tw W once, thro 5 more prs, ts with next pr, return thro 5 prs, tw W once, thro 3 more prs, tw W twice, edge st and pin) rep twice more.

Right side:
    Work in similar manner to lt side.*

Rep from * to * for desired length.

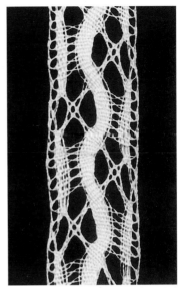

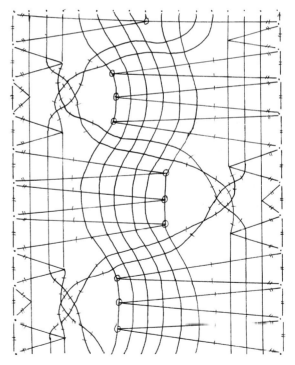

Meander with Spider

16 prs

Work in cls throughout.

Work ts with W and 8th passive pr from lt. Both these prs are now Ws and work out to each edge: the lt W thro 7 prs to lt, tw twice, edge st and pin; and the rt W thro 5 prs to rt, tw twice, edge st and pin. Leave.

Work 5th passive pr from lt thro 4 prs to rt, tw once. Leave.

Work 4th passive pr from lt thro same 4 prs to rt, tw once. Leave.

Left side:
 * Work W thro 3 prs, tw W once, thro 3 more prs, ts with next pr, return to lt with lt pr thro 3 prs, tw W once, thro 3 more prs, tw W twice, edge st and pin.*
 Rep from * to * once more.
 Work W thro 2 prs, ts with next pr, tw rt pr once, and return to lt with lt pr thro 2 prs, tw W twice, edge st and pin.
 Work W thro 2 prs, tw once. Leave.

Right side:
 Work W thro 2 prs to lt, ts with next pr. Tw lt pr once and return with rt pr thro 2 prs, tw W twice, edge st and pin. W thro 2 prs, tw once.
 † The spider is made with these 2 prs, which are twisted once, and the next 2 prs to the lt which are also twisted once.

To work spider:
 Lt 2 prs thro rt 2 prs, then outside lt pr thro next pr to rt, outside rt pr thro next pr to lt, cls with 2 centre prs, tw all 4 prs once.
 No pin is used. Pull up carefully. 2 lt prs are worked thro 4 prs to lt, tw both prs once. Leave.
 Of the remaining spider legs, work the rt one thro 2 prs to rt, tw twice, edge st and pin. Return thro 2 prs.
 Take the remaining spider leg and work ts with next pr to the rt, thro 2 more prs, tw twice, edge st and pin.

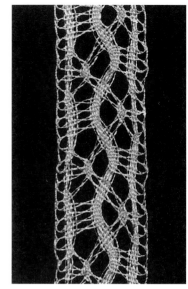

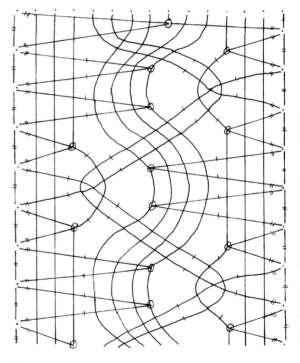

** Return thro 3 prs, tw once, thro 3 more prs, ts with next pr. Return with rt pr thro 3 prs, tw once, thro 3 more prs, tw twice, edge st and pin.**

Rep from ** to ** once more.

Work W thro 2 prs, ts with next pr, tw lt pr once and return to rt with rt pr thro 2 prs, tw W twice, edge st and pin.

Work W thro 2 prs, tw once. Leave.

Left side:

Work in similar manner to right side, beginning with a spider.[†]

Rep from [†] to [†] for desired length.

Mesh 1

16 prs

W should be on the rt of braid.

* W thro 2 prs in cls, tw W once, W thro next pr in cls and tw. (W thro next 2 prs in cls, tw all 3 prs once) rep 3 more times, W thro next 2 prs in cls, tw W twice, edge st and pin. Return thro 2 prs in cls, tw W once. Leave. (Work cls with the next 2 prs to the rt) rep 3 more times. Work next pr in cls thro 2 prs to the rt, tw W twice, edge st and pin.*

Rep from * to * for desired length.

To finish: work the W from lt to rt in cls.

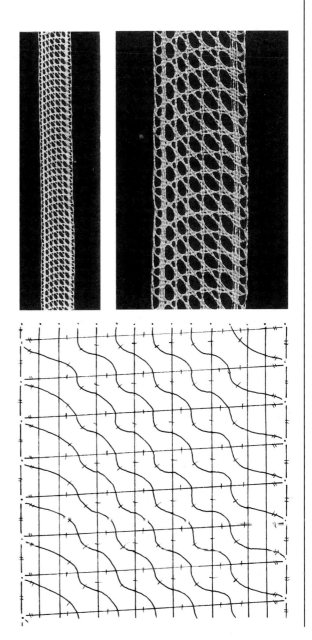

Mesh 2

16 prs

Work ts with W and centre pr. Both these prs are now Ws. Work lt W thro 6 prs to lt in cls, tw W twice, edge st and pin. Return thro 2 prs, tw W once. Leave. Work rt W to rt in similar manner.

Counting from the lt: work 7th pr to the lt cls and tw thro 3 prs, cls thro 2 prs, tw W twice, edge st and pin. Return thro 2 prs, tw W once. Leave. (Next 2 prs: cls and tw. Leave) twice.

Counting from the lt: work 11th pr to the lt cls and tw thro 7 prs, cls thro 2 prs, tw W twice, edge st and pin. Return thro 2 prs, tw W once. Leave. (Next 2 prs cls and tw. Leave) rep 3 more times. Next pr (4th pr from rt) works to the lt cls and tw thro 9 prs, cls thro 2 prs, tw W twice, edge st and pin. Return thro 2 prs, tw W once. Leave.

* (Next 2 prs cls and tw. Leave) rep 3 more times. Counting from the rt: work 4th pr to the rt thro 2 prs, tw W twice, edge st and pin. Return thro 2 prs, tw W once, cls and tw thro 9 prs, cls thro 2 prs, tw W twice, edge st and pin. Return thro 2 prs, tw W once. Leave.*

Rep from * to * for desired length.

To finish: the diagonal Ws leave 2 twisted prs unworked until the braid is level.

Variation 3

This is started in the same way as Mesh 2, but the working method differs in two respects:
    The passive prs are crossed in cls only (no tw).
    The W is worked thro both prs in cls, then tw once all 3 prs.

Variation 4

This is started in the same way as Mesh 2, but the working method differs in two respects:
    The passive prs are crossed in cls only (no tw).
    The W works thro both prs in cls. Tw W once, then cls and tw with the 2 prs passed thro.

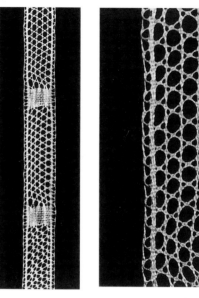

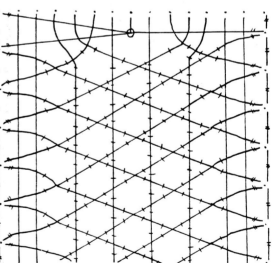

Mesh 2, 3 and 4

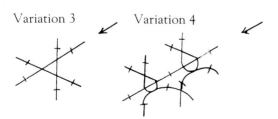

Open Spider

16 prs

Work ts with W and centre pr. Both these prs are now Ws. Work lt W to lt thro 6 prs, tw W twice, edge st and pin. Leave. Work rt W to rt in similar manner. Leave.

* Left side:
　　W thro 6 prs.
　　† Tw W twice, leave, and return to lt with last pr passed thro, tw W twice, edge st and pin.†
　　W thro 5 prs. Rep from † to †
　　W thro 4 prs. Rep from † to †
　　W thro 3 prs. Rep from † to †
　　W thro 2 prs, tw W twice. Leave.

Right side:
　　Work in similar manner to lt side.

Centre 8 prs for open spider:
　　Work lt 4 prs thro rt 4 prs.
　　Work 4th pr from lt thro 3 prs, ts with next pr, return to lt thro 3 prs, tw W twice, thro 2 more prs, tw W twice, edge st and pin. Leave.
　　Work 4th pr from rt thro 3 prs, ts with next pr, return to rt thro 3 prs, tw W twice, thro 2 more prs, tw W twice, edge st and pin. Leave.
　　Work lt 4 prs thro rt 4 prs. Tw each pr twice. Leave.

Left side:
　　W thro 3 prs. Rep from † to †
　　W thro 4 prs. Rep from † to †
　　W thro 5 prs. Rep from † to †

Right side:
　　Work in similar manner to lt side.*

Rep from * to * for desired length.

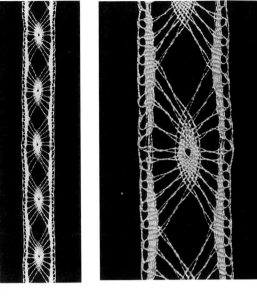

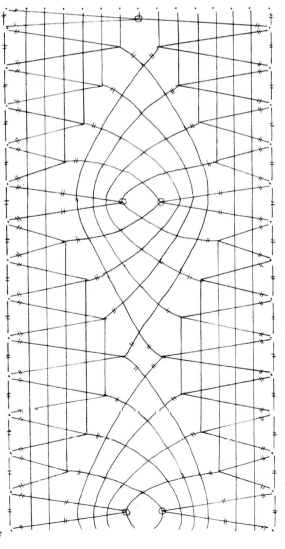

Orchid 1

16 prs

Work ts with W and centre pr. Both these prs are now Ws. Work lt W to the lt thro 6 prs, tw W twice, edge st and pin. Leave. Work rt W to rt in similar manner.

* Centre 4 prs.
    Work 2 lt prs thro 2 rt prs in cls.

Left side:
    W thro 4 prs, tw W once, thro 2 more prs. Leave.

Right side:
    Work in similar manner to lt side.

Cls Ws in the centre. The Ws have now changed sides.

Left side:
    Work lt W thro 2 prs, tw W once, thro 4 prs, tw W twice, edge st and pin. Return thro 4 prs. Tw W and next 2 prs once and work W thro these 2 prs in cls and tw. Work the lt of these 3 prs to the lt thro 4 prs in cls, tw twice, edge st and pin. Return thro 4 prs, tw W once, cls and tw with next pr. Return with the lt of these 2 prs thro 4 prs, tw W twice, edge st and pin. Leave.

Right side:
    Work in similar manner to lt side.*

Rep from * to * for desired length.

Finish with the centre crossing of 4 prs, then work ts with both Ws. Leave 1 as a passive and continue with the remaining W.

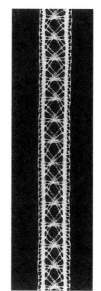

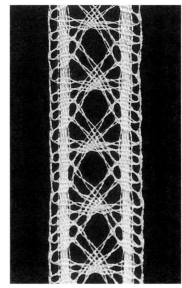

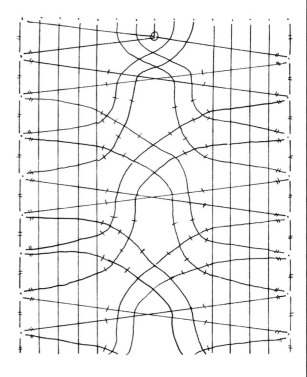

Orchid 2

16 prs

Work ts with W and centre pr. Both these prs are now Ws. Lt W thro 6 prs to lt in cls, tw W twice, edge st and pin. Rt W to rt in similar manner.

Centre 4 prs:
   * 2 lt prs cls.
   2 rt prs cls.
   Work 2 lt prs thro 2 rt prs in cls.

Left side:
   Work W thro 4 prs in cls, tw W once, thro 2 more prs. Leave.

Right side:
   Work in similar manner to lt side.

Cls Ws in the centre. The Ws have now changed sides.

Left side:
   Lt W thro 2 prs to lt, tw W once, thro 4 more prs, tw W twice, edge st and pin. Return thro 4 prs, tw W and next 2 prs once, W thro next pr cls and tw. Return with lt pr as new W, thro 4 prs, tw W twice, edge st and pin. **Leave.**

Right side:
   Work in similar manner to lt side.*

Rep from * to * for desired length.

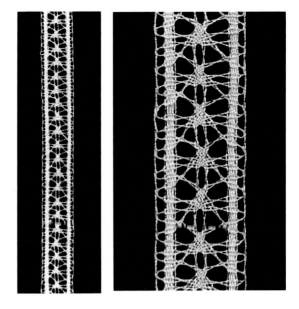

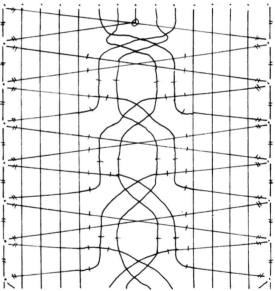

Orchid 3

16 prs

Work ts with W and centre pr. Both these prs are now Ws. Work lt W to lt in cls thro 6 prs, tw W twice, edge st and pin. Return thro 2 prs, tw W once. Leave. Work rt W to rt in similar manner.

* Centre 4 prs:

Work 2 lt prs in cls thro 2 rt prs. Work cls with 2 lt prs. Work cls with 2 rt prs. Tw all 4 prs once.

Left side:

Work 7th pr from lt to the lt thro 2 prs, tw W once, thro next pr in cls and tw, thro 2 more prs, tw W twice, edge st and pin. Return thro 2 prs, tw W once. Leave this pr and take next pr to rt (which has 1 tw) and work thro 2 prs to rt, tw W once, thro next pr in cls and tw. Return with the lt of these 2 prs thro 2 prs, tw W once, thro next pr in cls and tw, thro 2 more prs, tw W twice, edge st and pin. Return thro 2 prs, tw W once. Leave this pr and take next pr to rt (which has 1 tw) and work thro 2 prs to rt, tw W once. Leave.

Right side:

Work in similar manner to lt side.*

Rep from * to * for desired length.

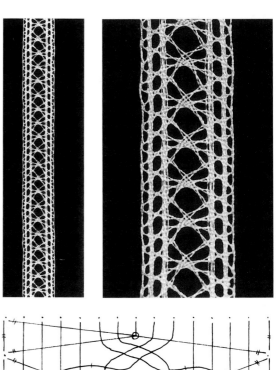

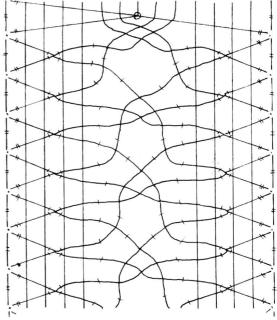

Orchid 4

16 prs

Work ts with W and centre pr. Both these prs are now Ws. Work lt W to lt in cls thro 6 prs, tw W twice, edge st and pin. Return thro 4 prs, tw W once. Leave. Work rt W to rt in similar manner.

* Centre 2 prs:
    Tw each pr twice and work 3 half-stitches.

Centre 4 prs:
    Tw the 2 outside prs once.
    Work cls and tw with 2 lt prs.
    Work cls and tw with 2 rt prs.
    Work cls with 2 centre prs.

Left side:
    Work W (6th pr from lt) to centre: cls and tw thro 1 pr and cls thro next pr.

Right side:
    Work in similar manner to lt side.

Two Ws (centre prs) work cls. Both Ws have now changed sides.

Left side:
    Lt W to lt: cls thro 1 pr, tw W once, cls and tw thro next pr, cls thro 4 prs, tw W twice, edge st and pin. Return thro 4 prs, tw W once, cls thro next pr. Take the lt of these 2 prs as new W, tw it once and work to lt thro 4 prs, tw W twice, edge st and pin. Return thro 4 prs, tw W once. Leave.

Right side:
    Work in similar manner to lt side.*

Rep from * to * for desired length.

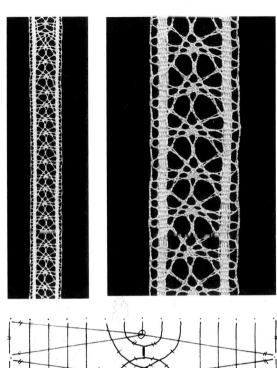

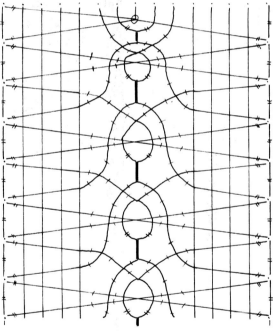

Periwinkle

16 prs

Work in cls throughout. Work ts with W and centre pr. Both these prs are now Ws. Work lt W thro 6 prs to lt, tw W twice, edge st and pin. Leave. Work rt W to rt in similar manner.

Centre 6 prs:

Lt pr thro 1 pr to rt, ts with next pr, return with lt pr thro 1 pr. Leave.

Rt pr thro 1 pr to lt, ts with next pr, return with rt pr thro 1 pr. Leave.

Work the 2 centre lt prs thro the 2 centre rt prs.

Tw all 6 prs twice.

* Left side:

Counting from the lt, including edge pr:

Work 6th pr to lt thro 3 trail prs, tw W twice and work thro next pr. Leave.

Work 7th pr to lt thro 3 trail prs, tw W twice, work thro 2 more prs, tw W twice, edge st and pin. Leave.

Work 8th pr to lt thro 2 trail prs, ts with next pr, return with rt pr, thro 2 trail prs, tw W twice. Leave.

Work 2nd pr from lt thro 2 prs, tw W twice, thro 3 trail prs, tw W twice. Leave.

Work the 2nd and 3rd prs from lt in cls and tw both prs twice. Work the rt of these 2 prs thro 3 trail prs to rt, tw W twice. Leave.

Work the 2nd pr from lt thro edge pr and pin.

Work the rt of these 2 prs thro 2 trail prs to rt, ts with next pr. Return with lt pr thro 2 trail prs, tw W twice, edge st and pin. Leave.

Right side:

Work in similar manner to lt side.

Open spider with centre 6 prs:

† 2 centre lt prs thro 2 centre rt prs.

Outside lt pr thro 1 pr to rt, ts with next pr, return with lt pr thro 1 pr.

Outside rt pr thro 1 pr to lt, ts with next pr, return with rt pr thro 1 pr.†

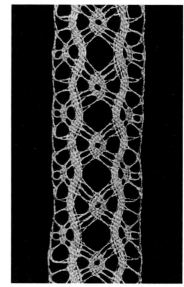

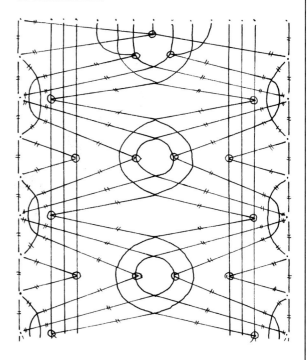

2 centre lt prs thro 2 centre rt prs.

Tw all 6 prs twice.*

Rep from * to * for desired length.

To finish, work the open spider from † to †. Work Ws (second pr from lt and second pr from rt) to centre and make ts. Turn diagram upside down for working method to finish.

Ricrac

19 prs

* Work 4 rows of cls, finishing with W on lt. Leave edge pr and W on lt. Tw twice next 2 prs of passives. Leave.

† Next 4 prs: pass lt 2 prs thro rt 2 prs in cls, tw each pr twice. Leave.†

Rep from † to † twice more.

Tw twice last 2 passive prs. Leaving the rt edge pr and working from the rt, rep from † to † 4 times.*

Rep from * to * for desired length.

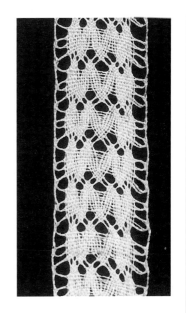

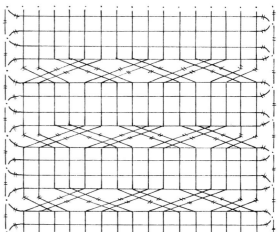

Ripples

16 prs

Work in cls throughout.

Work ts with W and centre pr. Both these prs are now Ws. Work lt W to the lt thro 6 prs, tw W twice, edge st and pin. Work rt W to the rt in a similar manner. Leave.

* Left side:
   W thro 4 prs, tw W twice, thro 4 more prs, tw W twice, thro 3 more prs, ts with next pr. Return with lt pr thro 3 prs, tw W twice, thro 4 prs, tw W twice, thro 4 more prs, tw W twice, edge st and pin.
   W thro 4 prs, tw W twice, thro 3 prs, ts with next pr.
   Return with lt pr, thro 3 prs, tw W twice, thro 4 more prs, tw W twice, edge st and pin.
   W thro 3 prs, ts with next pr. Return with lt pr thro 3 prs, tw W twice, edge st and pin. Leave.

Right side:
   W thro 3 prs, ts with next pr. Return with rt pr thro 3 prs, tw W twice, edge st and pin. W thro 4 prs, tw W twice, thro 3 prs, ts with next pr. Return with rt pr thro 3 prs, tw W twice, thro 4 more prs, tw W twice, edge st and pin. W thro 4 prs, tw W twice, thro 4 more prs, tw W twice, thro 3 more prs, ts with next pr. Return with rt pr thro 3 prs, tw W twice, thro 4 more prs, tw W twice, thro 4 more prs, tw W twice, edge st and pin. Leave.*

Rep from * to * for desired length.

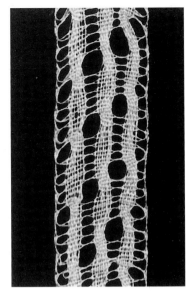

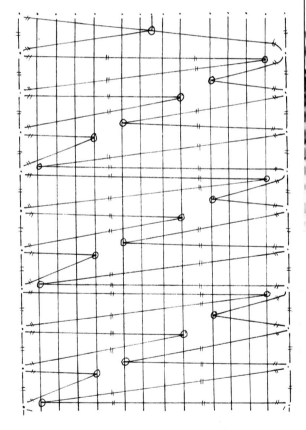

Roundel 1

16 prs

Work in cls throughout.

Work a ts with W and centre pr. Both these prs are now Ws. Work the lt W to the lt thro 4 prs, tw twice, thro 2 more prs, tw twice, edge st and pin. Leave. Work the rt W to the rt in a similar manner. Leave.

* Centre 4 prs:
   Work the lt 2 prs thro the rt 2 prs in cls. Leave.

Left side:
   † Work W thro 2 prs, tw W twice, W thro 3 more prs, work a ts with the next pr.
   Return with the lt of these 2 prs, thro 3 prs, tw W twice, thro 2 more prs, tw W twice, edge st and pin.†
   Rep from † to † twice more.

Right side:
   Work in a similar manner as lt side.*

Rep from * to * for desired length.

Note   If a thicker thread is being used on a wider braid, it may be better to twist once instead of twice between the passive prs.

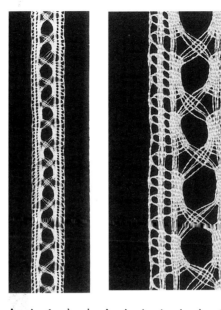

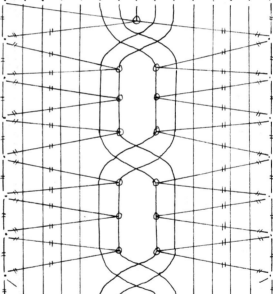

Roundel 2

16 prs

Work ts with W and centre pr. Both these prs are now Ws. Work lt W thro 4 prs to lt, tw W twice, thro 2 more prs, tw W twice, edge st and pin. Leave. Work rt W to rt in a similar manner.

* Centre 4 prs:
   2 lt prs cls. 2 rt prs cls.
   Work 2 lt prs thro 2 rt prs.
   2 lt prs cls. 2 rt prs cls.

Left side:
   (Work W thro 2 prs, tw W twice, thro 3 prs, ts with next pr, return with lt pr thro 3 prs, tw W twice, thro 2 prs, tw W twice, edge st and pin) rep once more. Leave.

Right side:
   Work in similar manner to lt side.*

Rep from * to * for desired length.

Variation

The centre 4 prs may be twisted and worked with a cls and tw, and the crossing made like a windmill, i.e. using 2 bobbins together as 1 thread. This gives a tighter appearance.

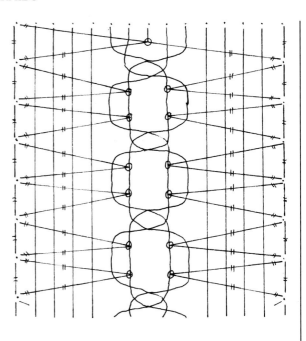

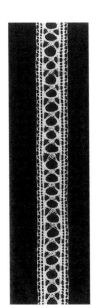 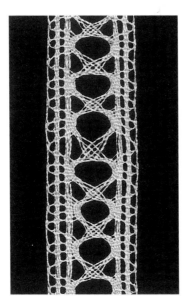

Running River

17 prs

Work ts with W and 7th passive pr from lt. Both these prs are now Ws. Work lt W to the lt thro 6 prs, tw W twice, edge st and pin, and close pin with inside pr cls and tw twice. Leave. Work rt W to rt thro 7 prs, tw W twice, edge st and pin, and close pin with inside pr cls and tw twice. W cls thro 3 prs to lt, tw W twice, thro 2 more prs, ts with next pr, return with rt pr thro 2 prs, tw W twice, thro 3 more prs, tw W twice, cls and tw twice, edge st and pin. Close pin with cls and tw twice. Leave.

* Left side:
   Work a 5 pr spider with prs 4, 5, 6, 7 and 8 from lt, in cls, following the diagram, making a ts with the prs that are ringed. On completion, pull up carefully; no pin is required. The 5 prs are then twisted twice.

Work the 4th pr from lt thro 3 prs to the lt in cls and tw twice, pin, and close pin.

Work the 5th pr from lt thro 4 prs to the lt in cls and tw twice, pin, and close pin.

Work the 8th pr from lt thro (3 prs to rt in cls, tw W twice) rep once more, thro the next 3 prs in cls and tw twice, pin, and close pin. Leave.

Work 7th pr from lt thro (3 prs to rt in cls, tw W twice) rep once more, thro the next 4 prs in cls and tw twice, pin, and close pin. Leave.

Work 6th pr from lt thro (3 prs to rt in cls, tw W twice) rep once more. Leave.

Then work the 5th and 4th prs thro in the same way.

Work the 3rd pr from lt thro 3 prs to rt in cls, tw W twice, thro 2 more prs, ts with next pr. Return with lt pr thro 2 prs, tw W twice, thro 3 prs, tw twice, thro next 2 prs in cls and tw twice, pin and close pin. Leave.

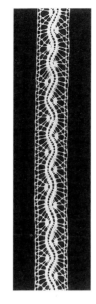

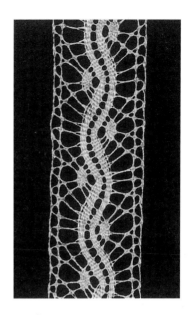

Lt Spider   Rt Spider

Right side:

Beginning with rt spider (see diagram) work in similar manner to lt side.*

Rep from * to * for desired length.

Finish with a spider on rt or lt and ts on the other side. Work Ws to centre and make ts, 1 pr continuing as W.

If too tight, the inner footside pr may have one twist or none at all.

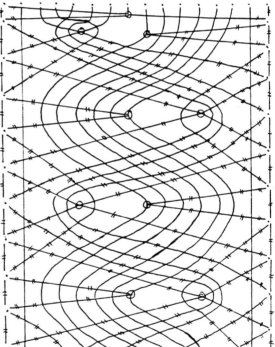

Sidesteps

16 prs

Work ts with the W and 8th passive pr from
lt. Both these prs are now Ws. Work lt W to lt
thro 3 prs, tw W once, thro 4 prs, tw W twice,
edge st and pin. Work rt W thro 5 prs to rt in
similar manner.

Left side:

Work W in cls thro 4 passive prs, tw W
once, cls thro next 2 prs and ts with next pr.
Tw rt of these 2 prs twice, and the lt pr works
another ts with the next pr to lt. Tw rt of these
2 prs twice, tw lt pr once and work it in cls
thro next pr, tw it once again, work it thro
remaining 4 passive prs, tw twice, edge st and
pin. Leave.

* Right side:

All passive prs worked in cls.

Work W thro 4 passive prs, tw W once,
thro next pr and ts with next pr (which has 2
twists).

Return with rt pr as W and work it thro
next pr, tw W once, thro 4 prs, tw W twice,
edge st and pin.

Return thro 4 prs, tw W once, thro 2 more
prs and ts with next pr (the 2nd pr which has 2
twists). Tw lt pr twice. With the rt pr work
another ts with next pr to rt, tw lt of these 2
prs twice, and tw rt pr once, work it thro 1 pr,
tw it once again, thro 4 prs, tw twice, edge st
and pin. Leave.

Left side:

Work in similar manner to right side.*

Rep from * to * for desired length.

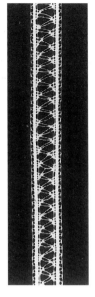
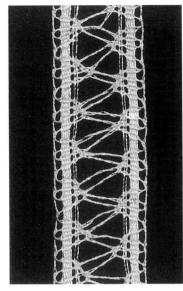
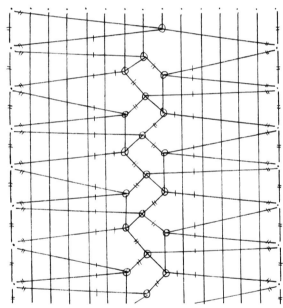

Stripes

16 prs

* Work 2 rows of cls, leaving W and edge pr on lt.

From the lt:
   (Next 2 prs of passives cls and tw) rep 5 more times, tw last pr passives once.

From the rt:
   Leave the rt edge pr. (Next 2 prs of passives work cls) rep 5 more times.*

Rep from * to * for desired length.

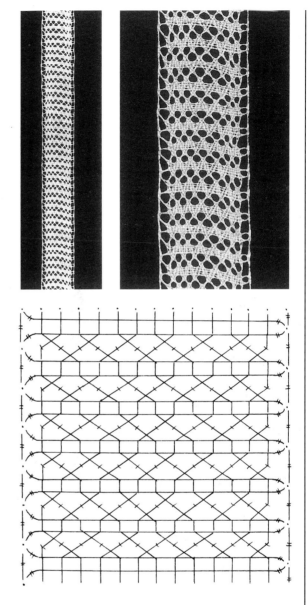

Waves

16 prs

Work in cls throughout. W from lt thro 1 pr, cls and tw. Leave.

From right side:

   3rd and 4th prs from rt, cls. Lt of these 2 prs (thro 3 prs to lt, tw W once) rep twice more, thro 1 pr. (These 2 prs will form the body of the little spider.) Leave.

   * Tw once 3rd pr from rt and work it to the rt thro 1 pr in cls and tw, tw W once more, edge st and pin. Return thro inner edge pr in cls and tw, then (thro 3 prs to lt, tw W once) rep once more, thro 2 prs, ts with next pr.

   With the lt of these 2 prs tw once, work thro 2 prs (for the little spider) tw W once, thro next pr, cls and tw, tw W once more, edge st and pin. Return thro inner edge pr cls and tw, thro 2 spider prs, tw W once. Leave.

   Take the next pr (which was the rt pr from the ts) and work it to the rt thro 2 prs, tw W once (thro 3 prs, tw W once) rep once more, thro 1 pr in cls and tw, tw W once more, edge st and pin. Return thro inner edge pr in cls and tw, then (thro 3 prs to lt, tw W once) rep once more, thro 2 prs, ts with next pr.

   Work the rt of these 2 prs thro 2 prs to rt, tw W once (thro 3 prs, tw W once) rep once more, thro 1 pr in cls and tw, tw W once more, edge st and pin. Return thro inner edge pr in cls and tw. Leave.

From left side:

   Beginning with 3rd and 4th prs from lt, cls and tw.

   Work rt of these 2 prs (thro 3 prs, tw W once) rep twice more. Work cls with next pr. Leave. (These 2 prs will form the body of the little spider.)

Now work in same way in reverse as rt side from *.

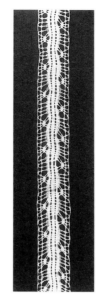
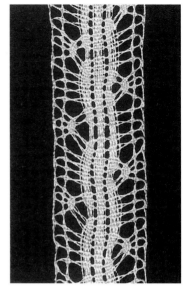
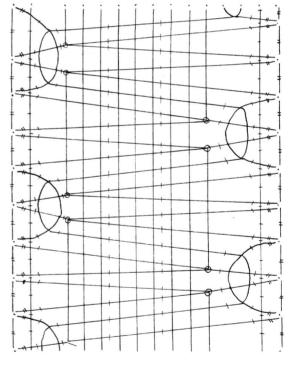

Spiral Braids

Ammonite

15 prs

The decoration in this braid will show best when the pattern is tightly curved, as here. Blind pins should be used as necessary when working the inside of the curve. These have been indicated on the sample pattern.

* Work 2 rows of cls. Leave W on *inside* of curve.

Tw twice 5 passive prs on outside of curve, tw once next 5 passive prs, leave untwisted the last 2 passive prs (on inside of curve).*

Rep from * to * for desired length.

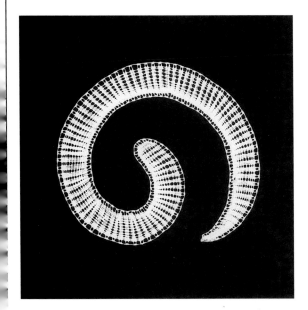

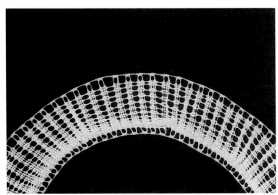

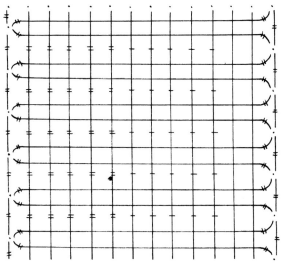

Inside curve

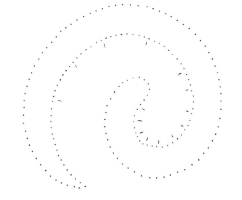

Chevron

16 prs

The decoration in this braid will show best when the pattern is tightly curved, as here. If possible, make twice as many pin holes on the outside of the curve (see the sample pattern).

Work a few rows of cls braid. Leave W as a passive pr in the centre. Tw twice the 5 passive prs on lt and the 5 passive prs on rt.

* Work the 2 centre lt prs thro the 2 centre rt prs in cls. Work the lt of the 4 centre prs in cls thro 5 prs to lt, tw W twice, edge st and pin. Leave.

Work the lt of the remaining 3 centre prs in cls thro 6 prs to lt, tw W twice, edge st and pin. Leave.

Work the rt of the 2 remaining centre prs thro 5 prs to rt, tw W twice. Leave.

Work the remaining centre pr thro 6 prs to rt, tw W twice, edge st and pin. Leave.

Tw all the passive prs twice.*

Rep from * to * for desired length.

Reverse these instructions if the inside of the curve is on the left.

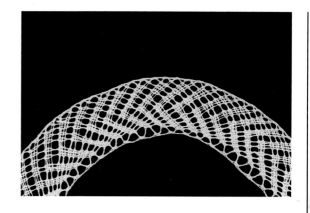

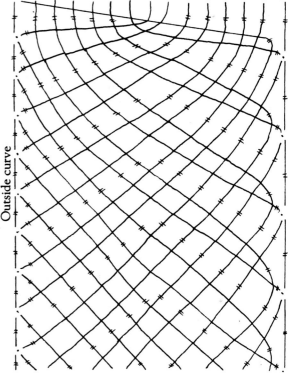

Outside curve

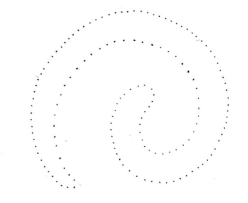

Additional Working Diagrams

Photographs and full instructions for these diagrams appear in our previous book *Milanese Lace*.

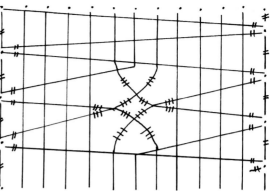

Four-pin Bud

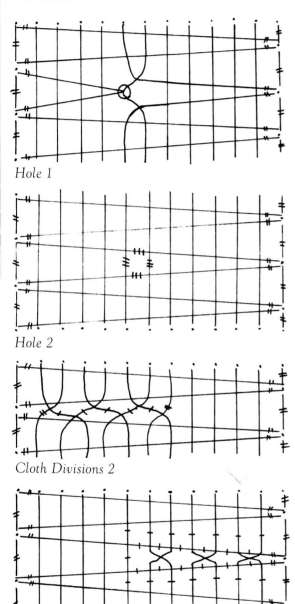

Hole 1

Hole 2

Cloth Divisions 2

Cloth Divisions 3

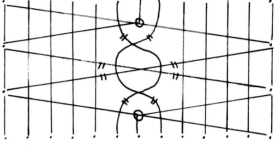

Maltese Spot

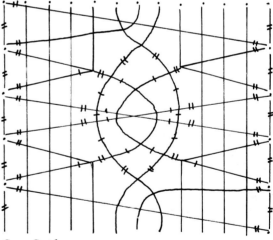

Spot Spider

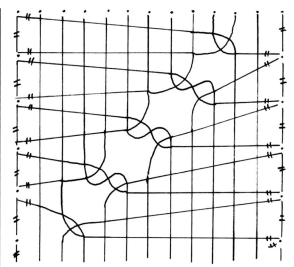

Zigzag Holes

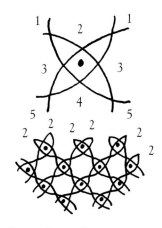

Cane Ground
Work all joins ws and twist.

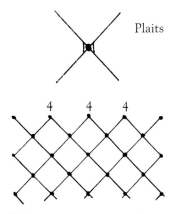

Plaits

Valenciennes
Work plaits with 4 hs. Joins are made with hs,
pin, hs.

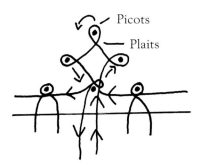

Picots
Plaits

Picot Edging

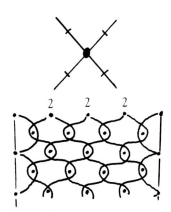

Tulle du Puy
Work all joins with cls, pin, cls and tw.

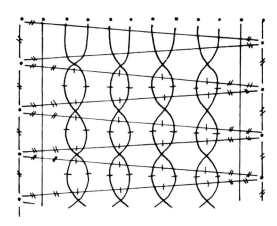

Ribbon
Work in cls throughout with twists as indicated.

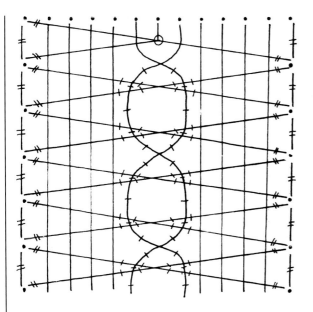

Ovals
Work in cls throughout with twists as indicated.

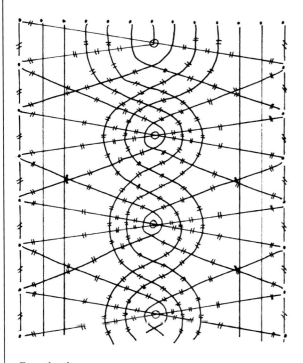

Pinwheel
Work in cls throughout with twists as indicated.
The Ws in the centre of the pinwheel may be
worked in cls instead of ts.

Plaits with Windmill Crossing

The crossing is made with a cls, using two bobbins together as one. Pin in the centre of the cls.

For those lacemakers who are accomplished in all the techniques used in the patterns in this book we recommend the following as an additional source of reference:

Milanese Lace: An Introduction by Patricia Read and Lucy Kincaid (Batsford)
The Book of Bobbin Lace Stitches by Bridget and Geraldine Stott (Batsford)
The Technique of Honiton Lace by Elsie Luxton (Batsford)

Scroll Method

14 prs

This method is used when making tight curves in braids. The following instructions are for working the outer curve on the left, and should be reversed when the outer curve is on the right.

Work the Ws thro 1 pr and tie 1 knot. Work Ws thro 1 more pr. Leave

There are 9 passive prs to the rt of the weavers; number them 1 to 9 from lt to rt. Work no. 1 passive pr thro 3 prs to the lt, tw twice, edge st and pin under 2 prs. Work back thro 2 prs only. Leave. Work no. 2 passive pr thro 4 prs to the lt, tw twice, edge st and pin

45

under 2 prs. Work back thro 2 prs only. Leave.

Continue in this manner, working:
  no. 3 passive pr thro 5 prs to lt
  no. 4 passive pr thro 6 prs to lt
  no. 5 passive pr thro 7 prs to lt
  no. 6 passive pr thro 8 prs to lt.

Work back each time from the edge st thro 2 prs only. Work no. 7 passive pr thro 9 prs to lt, tw twice, edge st and pin under 2 prs. Work back thro all the passive prs, including nos 8 and 9, tw twice, make the edge st.

Continue working in braid. More detailed instructions for working scrolls can be found on pp. 21–2 of *Milanese Lace*.

Links: A Filling

Four pin holes are used in diamond formation for each link. The sample grid has been marked on 2 mm. paper, as used for the Square Mat pattern on p. 101.

Eight prs are required for each link:
  Work each set of 2 prs in cls and tw.
  Centre 2 prs cls and tw. Pin between. Leave.
  Work cls with 2nd and 3rd prs from lt.
  Work the rt side in the same way.
  Work 3rd pr from lt thro next pr on rt in cls.
  Work 3rd pr from rt thro next pr on lt in cls.
  Cls with 2 centre prs.
  Divide work in half.

Left side:
  Rt pr cls thro 2 prs to lt. Leave lt pr.
  Cls with rt pr and next pr to rt.
  Cls st with lt of these 2 prs and next pr to lt.
  Tw lt pr twice and work it in cls thro next pr to lt. Tw lt pr once and rt pr twice and pin up as for edge st (i.e. under 2 prs) as in diagram.

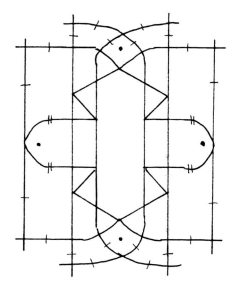

Right side:
  Work in same way as lt side.

Continue working in reverse order.

Note   Depending on the density of the work in relation to the space being filled and the thread used, one or two twists may be made where indicated. It is recommended that a sample is worked first.

CHAPTER TWO

The Patterns

Leaf Spray

Worked by Jenny Macpherson

Thread

Gassed cotton 100

Order of working

1   Set up on the circled holes and work the crescent shape to a point where the prs are gradually thrown out. The last few prs can be tied back or threads left to be sewn off when the next braid is worked.

2   Work each of the leaf sprays in turn, using top sewings where the work touches.

3   Filling.

Braids

Ammonite
Grenades

Filling

Cane Ground (p. 44)

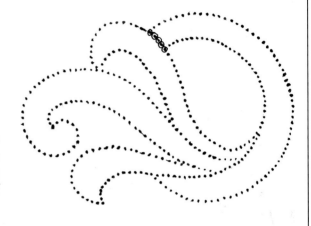

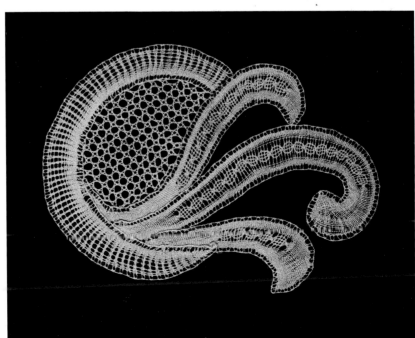

Scroll Motif

Designed and worked by Jacquie Tinch

Thread

Gassed cotton 70

Order of Working

1   The central braid, starting with the scroll, negotiating the curves using the scroll method, and tapering to a point.

2   Scroll (under the scallops), tapering into first braid.

3   Top scroll, tapering into first braid.

4   Scallops, starting on the outside and tapering down between the two scroll braids.

Braids

Periwinkle
Hole 1 (p. 43)
Cloth Divisions 2 (p. 43)

Peacock

Worked by Fiona Haywood

Thread

Gassed cotton 120

Order of Working

1   Start at the beak. Prs need to be added as the braid turns and continues down to the chest, where it divides into 3 sections.

2   Back section into 10-stick at the tail end.

3   Middle section is worked in the same way.

4   The breast section is worked in cls and tapers down to a point, where 7 prs can be turned and used to work the frame.

5   On completion of the frame the prs can be used again in the outer tail feather.

6   Work all the remaining tail feathers.

7   Four prs are used in the 10-stick for the comb on the head.

Braid

Cross-net

Note   The frame is cls with edge st on the inside and picot plaits on the outside (see p. 44).

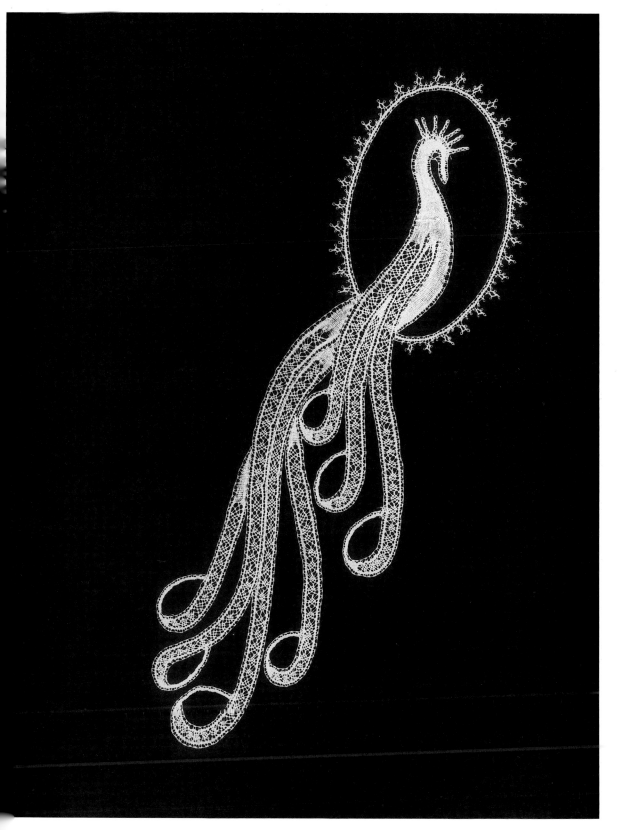

Shell

Worked by Katherine Timmins. (*See also full page photograph p. 130*)

Thread

Madeira Tanne 80

Order of Working

1   Begin with a scroll. When this section of braid is nearly finished put the prs aside.

2   Work the short cls braid across the middle, setting up at the blank end and sewing off into the existing braid. Then sew off the prs from the first braid.

3   Each braid in first half can now be worked in turn by sewing in and sewing off into existing work. Work second half by starting with the other scroll and completing to match first half. Final braid joins the two halves at the top of the shell.

4   Work 10-stick at the base of the fan, and fill this section with Ammonite (p. 41).

5   All fillings.

Braids

Roundel 2
Maltese Spot (p. 43)

Fillings

Lattice 3 and 1
Ammonite

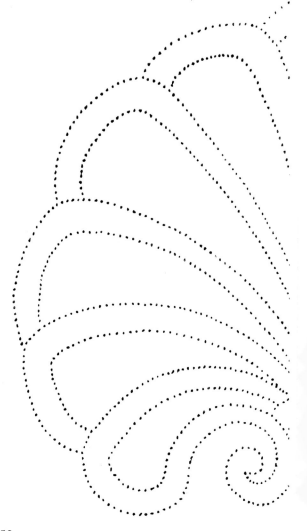

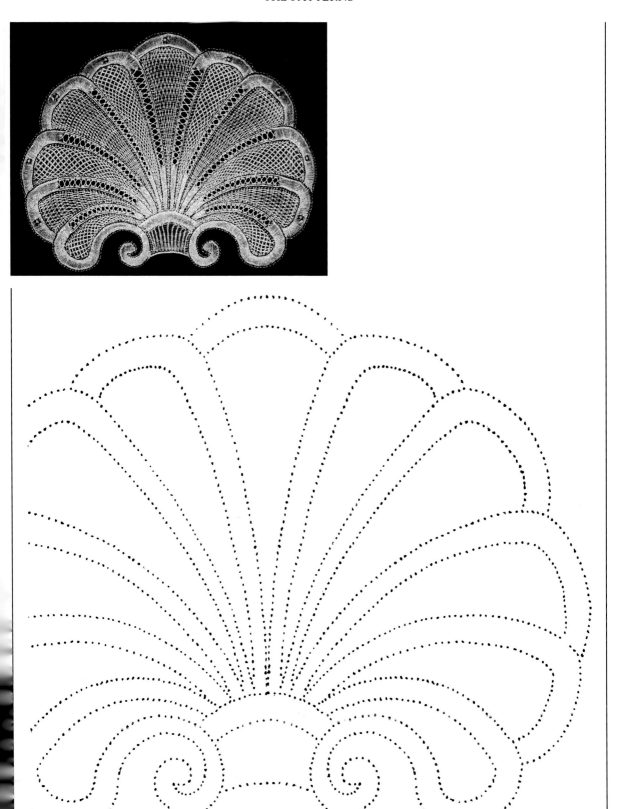

Leaf Circle

Designed and worked by Jane Read

Thread

Madeira Tanne 80

Order of Working

1   The braid is continuous, starting with the scroll. The first tight curve is worked by pricking holes across the corner and leaving the passives hanging at each hole, to be picked up again when the work is turned and the hole reused. The next point can be turned in the same way or using the scroll method.

2   Lattice 3 is used as a filling for the centre of the leaf.

Braids

Zigzag Holes (p. 44)
Meander with Rose
Fish 2   Note that more rows of cls have been worked between the fishes and several passive prs have been left on either side and worked in cls (the worker's own variation).

Note   Purl picots have been worked on the outside of the braid. These are optional.

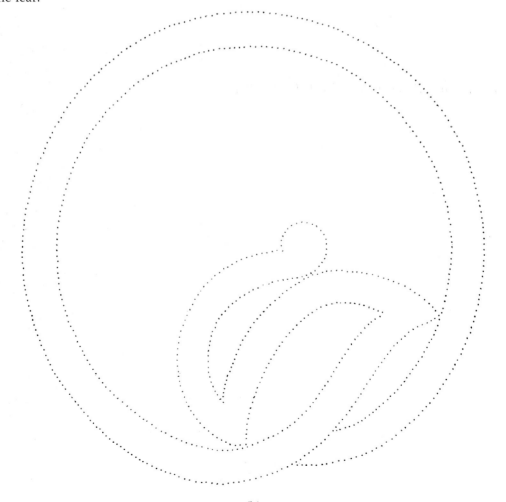

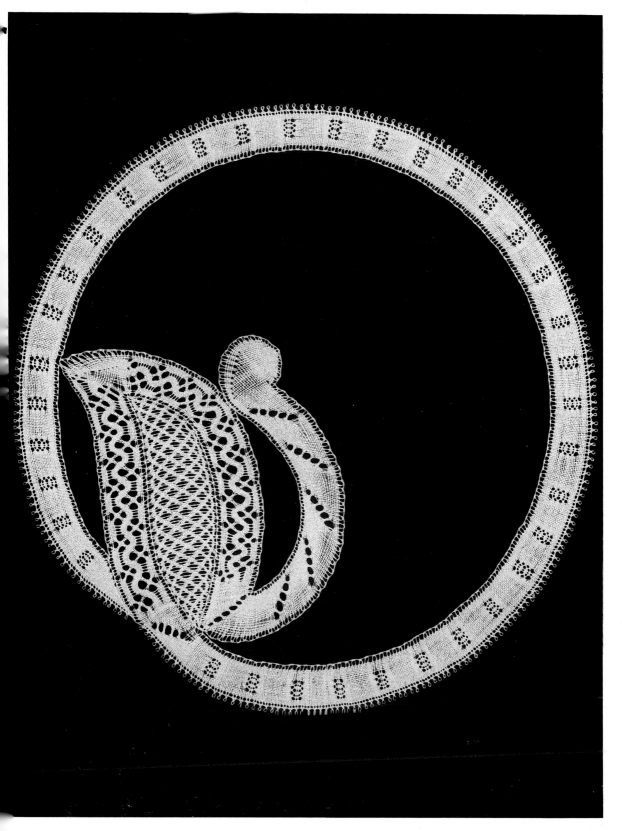

Basket

Worked by Fiona Haywood

Thread

Gassed cotton 120

Order of Working

1 Top and bottom rims of basket, from scroll to scroll.

2 Scalloped edge of the rims.

3 The braids of the basket, working from the top (wider end) to the bottom. Work the centre V-shape last.

4 Work the centre motif, which can be sewn into the basket at both ends of the braid.

5 Work each braid in turn so that it can be sewn into existing work.

Braids

Cloth Divisions (tw passive prs 3 times)
Hole 2 (p. 43)
Lattice 1
Grenades
Cross-net
Lotus 1
Meander with Ground

Snowball

Designed and worked by Jane Read

Thread

Copley Marshall 80

Order of Working

1. Each section begins with a scroll. To end the first scroll, either tie back the pairs or leave ends of thread to be sewn off later. Each succeeding scroll is then sewn off into the previous scroll.

2. Work all the fillings.

Braids

Lotus 1, 2 and 3
Lattice 1 and 2
Dewdrops
Ricrac
Grenades

Fillings

Mesh 2, 3 and 4
Hooked 1 and 2
Fish
Spiders
Lattice 3

Town Twinning:

Orpington, UK, and Huissen, The Netherlands

Buff Orpington

Designed by Tony Seppings and worked by Sheila Seppings

Thread

Madeira Tanne 80

Order of Working

1 The eye: work a ring of cls and fill with a haloed spider.

2 Into this braid work the comb and beak in hs.

3 Work neck feathers and wattle also into the eye braid.

4 Tail feathers: work a narrow 10-stick rib from the back neck feathers across the back to the start of the end tail feather. The work tapers to a point: either tie back these pairs or leave ends to be sewn off when the next feather is completed. The remaining 6 tail feathers begin at the bottom and sew off into the rib across the back.

5 The middle section of feathers: begin at the front end and sew off into the tail feather.

6 Front breast feathers.

7 Claws and legs.

Braids

Meander with Ground
Italian Spider
Lotus 1

Symbolic Bird (Huissen)

Design taken from the bronze statue in the town centre and worked by Sheila Seppings

Thread

Madeira Tanne 80

Order of Working

1 Head: 10-stick round the eye, along the top and down the back of the head, then turn the bobbins to fill in the head with cls. Beak starts at the point and sews off into head. Fill the eye with a tally.

2 Top braid from head to point of wing feather, where 6 prs of bobbins continue in 10-stick, to give a smooth outline to the feathers, and back into the wing. Sew off.

3 Wing braids, some of which are in hs.

4 Middle braid from tail to neck.

5 Three short cls braids between the last braid and the wing.

6 The outer braid is continuous from the head, down and up the leg and sews off into the body.

7 The under tail feather from tip to leg.

Braids

Four-pin Bud (p. 43)
Lotus 1 and 3
Holes 1

Oval Mat

Designed and worked by Jane Read

Thread

Madeira Tanne 80

Order of Working

This mat has 1 motif repeated 4 times.

1   Commence with scroll. On completing the circle shape, sew off a few pairs on the inside of the circle. The remainder can be worked in cls and continued into the leaf shape, adding a few pairs on the outside. The point of the leaf can be negotiated using the scroll method.

2   All fillings.

Braids

Meander with Ground
Meander with Spider

Fillings

Cane Ground (p. 44)
Valenciennes (p. 44)

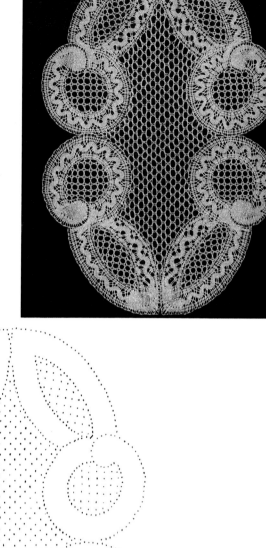

Bow

Thread

Madeira Tanne 80

Order of Working

1   Ten-stick round centre circle and overlay with cls.

2   Lower part of bow (both sides the same). Start at point on one side and follow braid right round and sew off into centre circle.

3   Work braids under this, on each side.

4   Bottom motif: begin and end with scroll.

5   Centre bud into this motif.

6   Top of bow: start and finish at each point.

7   Outer braid at top of bow and the leaves on each side.

8   The 2 outer circles of braid.

9   Fillings

Note   Steps 8 and 9 are optional. The bow will still look attractive if framed without these braids and fillings.

Braids

Daisy 2
Meander with Ground
Half-stitch
Ammonite
Cloth Divisions 3 (p. 43)

Filling

Torchon double ground: cls and tw, pin, cls and tw twice to close.

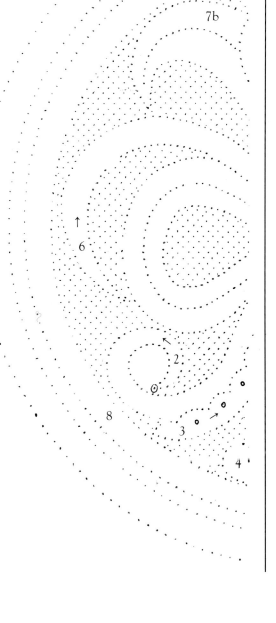

Cornucopia

Worked by Marjorie Ross. (*See also full page photograph p. 135*)

Thread

Gassed cotton 120

Order of Working

1   The central spine begins with the scroll and finishes at a point where the prs can be tied back.

2   The first braid to be worked starts on the outside of the scroll. The end tapers and is sewn off into the spine.

3   The next 4 braids on this side, each sewn into the existing work.

4   The last braid on this side starts with a scroll.

5   The braids on the other side of the scroll are worked in the same way, beginning with the braid under the first scroll.

6   Fillings.

Braids

Dewdrops
Hole 1 (p. 43)
Cloth Divisions (twist passive prs 3 times)

Fillings

Lattice 3
Lotus 2

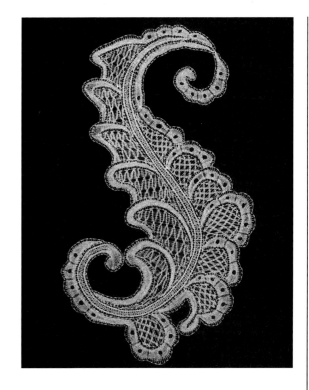

Shepherdess

Based on an illustration by the Russian illustrator Ivan Bilibin. Worked by Lucy Kincaid. (See also p. 112 and colour plate between pp. 112 and 113.)

Thread

Trident 60
Prick outline. Choose fillings and prick in with a finer pricker than the main outline.

Order of Working

1 Hair. Start with front lock.

2 Neckband.

3 Face. Work from neck upwards.

4 Ten-stick for outlines and folds. (See finished piece for where these occur.) Ten-stick folds on skirt optional.

5 Braids across back of apron and round cuffs.

6 Braids across lower apron.

7 Hand. Work from fingers towards cuff.

8 Stick.

9 Braids across hem of skirt.

10 Shoe.

11 Skirt, starting at hem each time and working up towards the waist.

12 Fillings.

Braids

Roundel 2 (without passives)
Lattice 3
Lattice 2
See also diagram

Fillings

Plaits with windmill crossings (p. 45)
Torchon ground: hs, pin, hs
Whole stitch ground with 1 twist

This is a free piece of lace. Pin holes can be added or left unworked as required.

If you are experimenting with colour, see pp. 110–12 first. Stencil Decor paints (available from most craft shops) were used by our lacemaker, but try whatever you have to hand. Test the colours and the way the fabric accepts the paint on a spare piece of braid worked in the same thread as the main work. If using stencil paints, dilute these very slightly by dampening the brush with water before dipping it into the paint. Do not overload the brush. Keep it relatively dry, and stroke the paint into the fabric. Take your time.

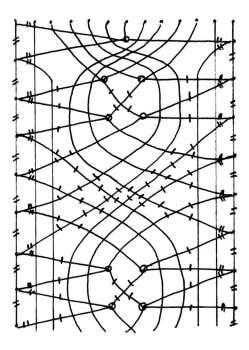

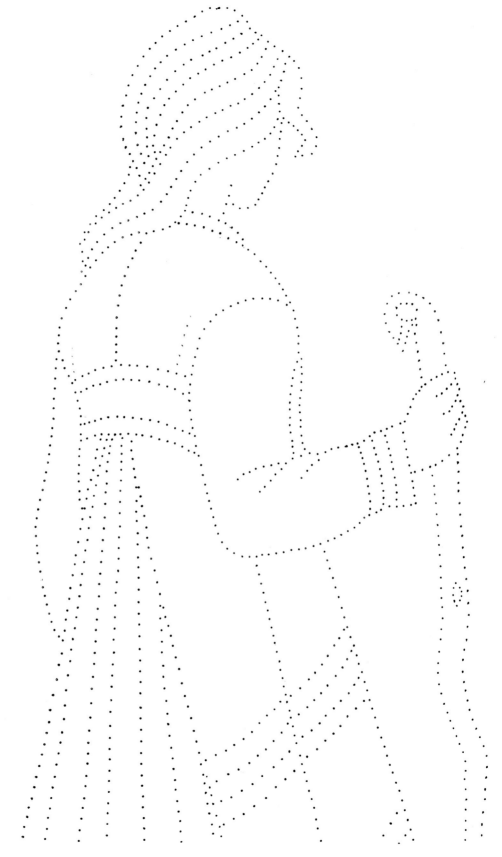

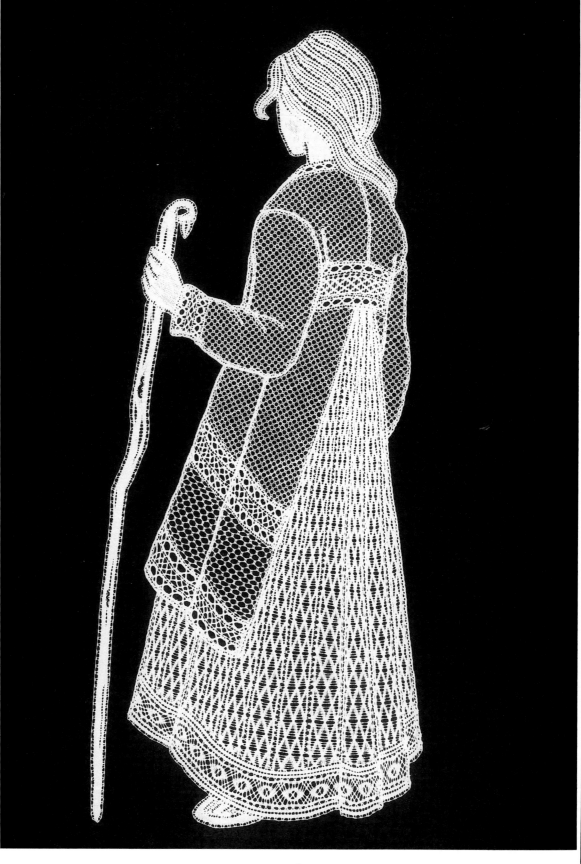

Rose Motif

Thread

Gassed cotton 120

Order of Working

1. Outer ring of flower, with scroll at each end.

2. Two inner braids of flower.

3. Trolley net fillings.

4. Stem, starting at point.

5. Second stem.

6. Lower leaf, starting at point.

7. Upper leaf.

Braids

Spot Spiders with Cloth Divisions (twist passive prs 3 times) (p. 43)

Cross-net
Fish 3

Fillings

Trolley Net (hs and 2 tw)

Fern Mat

Designed and worked by Jane Read

Thread

Madeira Tanne 80

Order of Working

This mat has 1 motif, complete in itself, repeated 4 times.

Commence with scroll, using the scroll method to negotiate points and curves. Reduce pairs down to the point when finishing

Braids

Hooked 2
Meander with Ground
Meander with Spider
Lattice 3
Cross-bud
Orchid 3

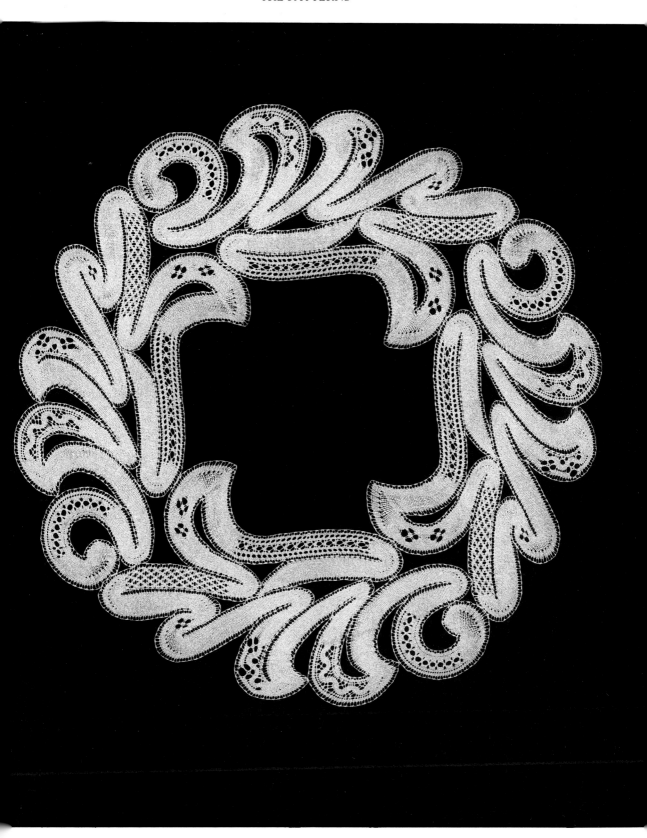

Rooster

Worked by Marjorie Ross

Thread

Gassed cotton 120

Order of Working

1 The head: work cls braid round the eye. Work a small circle of 10-stick for the ear and overlay with cls. Work the ear flap and sew into the ear. Work the 2 sections of hs, sewing off into the ear and the flap.

2 The beak, crest and wattle braids: from the outside and sew into the head.

3 Body feathers: begin with the back feather and sew into the head. Work the other feathers in turn, sewing off each one into existing work.

4 Claws and legs.

5 Tail feathers, beginning with the uppermost one.

Braids

Lotus 1   Dewdrops
Lattice 3 and 1 Half-stitch
Mesh 4

The coxcomb is a cls braid with 3 passive prs on one side, worked in cls and tw.

Jabot

Design taken from an old Milanese flounce. Worked by Kathleen Gidden. (*See also full page photograph p. 131*)

Thread

Madeira Tanne 80

Order of Working

Because the smaller piece is placed on top of the larger (the top bands are gathered with needle and thread), the central motif of the larger piece has been made with plain cls braid and simple filling.

1   The small motif is continuous and begins at the circled hole.

2   The straight band at the top.

3   All fillings.

4   The 2 halves of the larger piece are a mirror image. Work the straight band at the top.

5   The main braid begins in the centre and finishes where it started.
    Work the other side to match.

6   All fillings.

Braids

Maltese Spot (p. 43)
Cloth Divisions 2 (tw passives 3 times) and 3 (p. 43)
Hole 2 (p. 43)
Four-pin Bud (p. 43)
Lattice 3
* Lazy Tongs
The worker's own variation of Chevron.

Fillings

Valenciennes (p. 44)
Plaits with windmill crossings (p. 5)
Torchon ground (cls, pin, cls and tw to close)

* See p. 45 of *Milanese Lace* by Patricia Read and Lucy Kincaid or substitute a different braid.

Handkerchief

Designed and worked by Jane Read

Thread

Madeira Tanne 80

Order of Working

1 Commence at the ringed holes. The greater part of the pattern is continuous, with the scroll method used to get round the curves.

2 Work the smaller braids on each side of the corner motif.

3 Work the fillings.

4 The narrow edging starts and ends with a scroll. The scrolls can be attached to the main motif with sewings or can be joined with needle and thread when applied to material.

The corner can be used on its own and applied to a rolled-edge handkerchief.

Braids

Meander with Ground
Roundel 2
Running River

Fillings

Valenciennes (p. 44)

Celtic Swan

Designed and worked by Jane Read

Thread

Copley Marshall 80

Order of Working

1 The two parts of the beak are started separately. Join up to continue the braid round to the tail, where the work is finished at a point. It will be seen that extra pairs are needed for the wide part of this braid, which is worked in cls. Keep the work as flat as possible on the curve.

2 Start the crest at the outer tip. Work down to the top of the head. Change to cls for the eye, scrolling round the curve before sewing off into the braid.

3 Work the top outer braid.

4 Work the middle braid as a filling.

Braids

Cross-net	Lattice 2
Lotus 1	Lotus 2
Ricrac	Lattice 1
Meander with Ground	

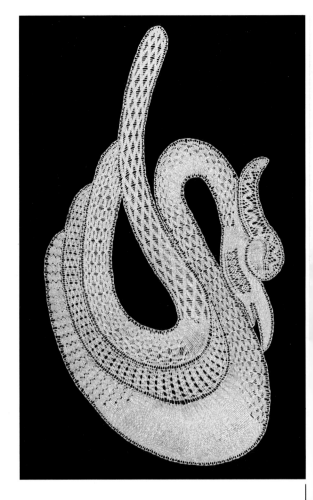

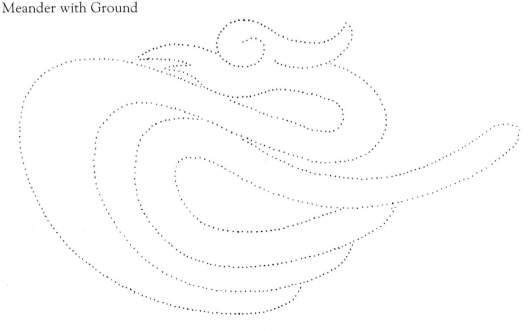

Serpents

Designed by Jane Read and worked by Marjorie Ross (*See also full page photograph on frontispiece*)

Thread

Gassed cotton 120

Order of Working

The two halves are a mirror image, except for the small leaf shape at the bottom, which is worked last. Begin at the tip of the large leaf shape, working the scalloped side first. When the braid has nearly reached the top of its section, put the prs aside and sew them off when the next section of the work is finished.

Follow the numbers in order as marked on the pattern.

Braids

   Maltese Spot (p. 43)
   Running River
   Daisy 2
   Lattice 1
   Hole 1 (p. 43)

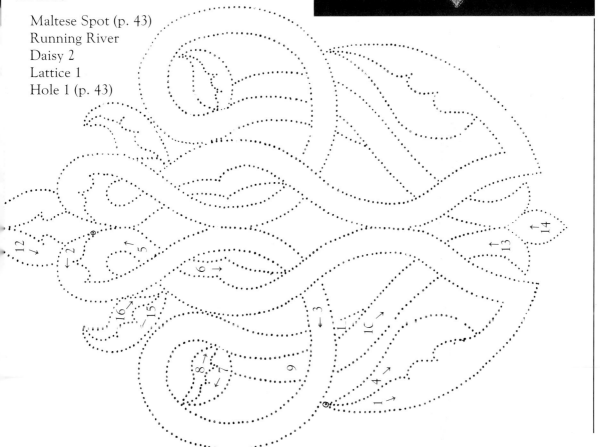

Gander and Geese

Designed and worked by Freda Bull

Thread

Gassed cotton 80

Order of Working

Gander

1   Commence with the 'up and down' cls braid with holes and divisions at the base and back of the neck. Work the back feathers into this braid.

2   Beak: start at the point, making a small breathing hole in the upper beak. Work both sets of beak prs into the head and neck braid.

3   Make a hole for the eye.

4   The braid to the tail turns at the point and becomes very narrow. The last few prs are sewn into the upper tail feather.

5   Claws and legs: the line of dots near the top of the legs indicates that the passives should be twisted twice. Complete the leg in cls and sew off into the body.

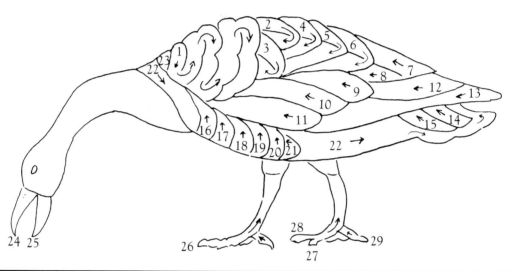

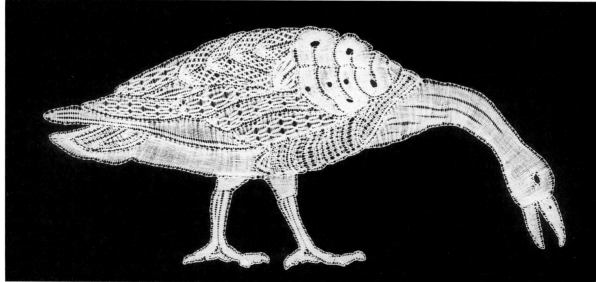

Geese

These are worked in the same way as the gander. The lower beak can be started at the point, turned and then tapered towards the top of the head. Take the last few prs into the head and neck braid. The upper beak is made next and sewn into the lower beak. (*See also full page photograph p. 132*)

Braids

Hole 1 (p. 43)
Cloth Divisions 2 (p. 43)
Lattice 3
Lotus 2
Dewdrops

Finial

Designed by Jane Read and worked by Marjorie Ross. (*See also full page photograph p. 133*)

Thread

Gassed cotton 120

To Work

The main (outer) part of this motif begins and ends with a scroll. The inner section is continuous and can be started in a cls section, while the curves are negotiated using the scroll method.

Braids

Roundel 2
Running River
Spot Spider (p. 43)
Lotus 1

Mask

Thread

Madeira Tanne 80

Order of Working

1 Lower lip with scroll at each end.

2 Upper lip.

3 Eyes and nose are worked continuously, with a scroll at each inner eye.

4 Ears and hair are worked continuously, beginning and ending with scrolls and using the scroll method (see p. 45) round the nose. To give emphasis to the nose 4 prs were added to work 10-stick on the upper (outer) curve before working the nose using the scroll method.

5 Chin to ear on each side.

6 Fillings.

Braids

Ammonite (p. 41)
Sidesteps
Cross-net
Dewdrops

Fillings

Mesh 1.

Flounce

Design taken from an old Milanese flounce. Worked by Bobbie Kilpatrick.

Thread

Madeira Tanne 80

Order of Working

This piece can be used as a jabot, and a straight braid has therefore been worked along the top to enable the lace to be gathered. This strip should be made last so that if it becomes worn through use it can easily be replaced.

In typical Milanese style the motifs are continuous and convoluted. The scroll method can be used to negotiate the curves. Turning stitch can be used in conjunction with this to create small holes at the ends of leaves. These holes are a feature of Milanese lace but care should be taken not to let them become too big.

The work begins and ends in three places, as marked on the pattern.

Braids

Spot Spider (p. 43)
Running River
Meander with Ground
Four-pin Bud (p. 43)
Lotus 1

Fillings

Plaits with Windmill Crossings
Cane Ground (p. 44)

Arcuate Mat

Winner of the John Bull Trophy, the Richard J. Viney Trophy and the Alison J. Fenney Trophy 1993. Joint winner of the Individuals Trophy 1993.

Designed and worked by Jane Read

Thread

Madeira Tanne 80

Order of Working

This mat consists of one motif repeated four times.

1   Start at the tip of the lower leaf. The work is then continuous to the tip on the other side, where it narrows and most pairs are thrown out.

2   Continue with 4 prs to the next tip: these will be the 2 edge prs, the weavers and 1 pr of passives.

3   To negotiate the deep points of the arch, prick pin holes across the corner and leave pairs hanging at each. These pairs can then be picked up again and the pin hole reused when the work is turned.

Braids

Meander with Ground
Orchid 1
Running River

Filling

Cane Ground (p. 44)

Handkerchief

Thread

Gassed cotton 120

Order of Working

1 Start at a cls section and work decorative braids on the outer sections of the curve.

2 Purl picots may be worked on the outer braids. Do not work picots where the lace is to be stitched onto material.

One corner may be worked and used by itself on a rolled-edge handkerchief.

Braids

Hooked 1
Meander with Ground
Spot Spider (p. 43)

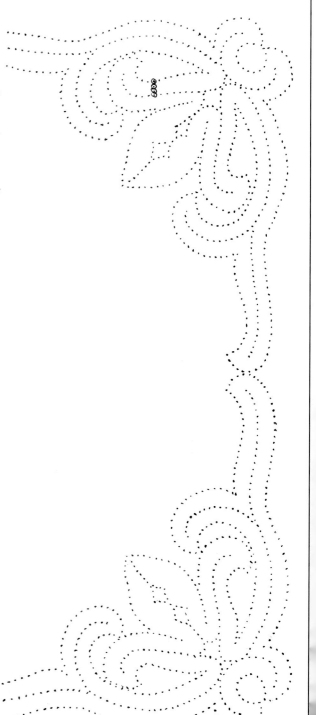

Turkey

Thread

Madeira Tanne 80

Order of Working

1   Inner ring of eye in 10-stick.

2   Outer ring of eye in cls.

3   Beak and tongue in cls, making a small hole in the upper beak.

4   Outline top knob and head in 10-stick. Overlay with hs.

5   Beard in hs.

6   Work the feathers to be sewn into the beard first. Each section of feathers can then be sewn off into the existing work.

7   Work the claw.

Braids

Ricrac
Chevron
Grenades
Lotus 1

Square Mat

Design taken from an old Milanese flounce.
Worked by Kathleen Gidden. (*See also full
page photograph p. 134*)

Thread

Madeira Tanne 80

To Work

The design contains one motif repeated four
times. Each motif begins and ends at the
centre point. The fillings are all added last.

Braids

Dewdrops
Maltese Spot (p. 43)
Daisy 1
Lattice 2 and 3
Lotus 3
Cross-net
Spot Spider (p. 43)

Fillings

Petals
Tulle de Puy (p. 44)
Links (see notes and diagrams, p. 46)

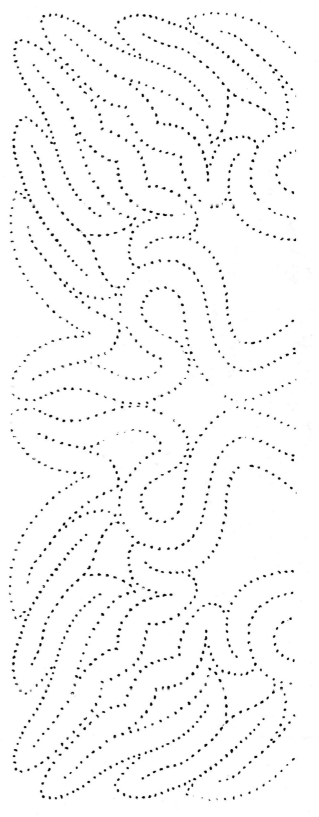

Collar

Worked by Bobbie Kilpatrick

Thread

Gassed cotton 120

Order of Working

The three main motifs have been adapted to fit the shape of the collar. The neckband should be worked last.

Picots may be made on the outside of the work, in which case an extra row of pin holes should be pricked round the outer edge of the pattern.

These holes are then used for the picots; they also serve to remind the worker where they start and finish.

1   Work the base of the first leaf shape.

2   The inner cls braid is worked before the 2 scalloped braids and the bobbins can then be turned and used for the zigzag braid up the side.

3   The 2 scalloped braids.

4   The filling.

5   The next leaf shape is continuous and commences at the scroll.

6   Flower shape. Work 10-stick round the central oval and overlay with cls. Work the 2 elongated shapes above and below this oval. The braids, starting with the scroll and ending at a point, should be worked next. All other braids are then worked in turn into the existing work.

7   All the motifs are worked in turn round the collar so that they can be joined with pillow sewings and the small connecting braids worked between the motifs.

Braids

Hole 1 (p. 43)
Cloth Divisions (tw passive prs 3 times)
Grenades
Lattice 3
Meander with Ground
Daisy 1

Filling

Cane Ground (p. 44)

Chimera (Winged Leopard)

Designed by Fay Read

Thread

Gassed cotton 120

Order of Working

1 Work the inner of the 2 forward (covert) wings, starting at the top and tying back the prs at the end.

2 Commence at top of outer eye with 5 prs and work 10-stick round the outside of the jaw. Leave the prs hanging to one side. These can be picked up and used with other prs from the side of the head for the braid down the neck.

3 Start the ears and top of the head, keeping the passives straight down to the jaw-line, where they can be sewn off with top sewings into the 10-stick. The eyes are worked with edge stitch. Weavers and 3 prs of passives are twisted twice for 4 rows at the point of the nose.

4 Outer of the two forward (covert) wings.

5 Work all the primary feathers, starting nearest the body. The legs and tail (steps 6–10) are all worked towards the body.

6 Where the braid narrows, 4 prs continue in 10-stick, and the outer prs continue the narrow braid until this also ends in 10-stick.

7 This braid also divides. The inner prs continue in braid and then in 10-stick. The outer prs work 10-stick until prs are added from a separate section of 10-stick. The prs continue in braid and are sewn off into the jaw.

8 The tail. Work from tip and sew into feathers, using 4 prs for 10-stick.

9 Rear leg. Braid divides: one section is worked into tail, the other into the body. The prs are finished off in 10-stick.

10 Rear leg. Braid divides: one section is worked into the other rear leg, while the other is worked along the underbelly and sewn off into the front leg.

11 Work any remaining curls of 10-stick.

12 Overlay the 10-stick with trolly net (hs and tw twice). No pin holes are needed for this. Work across from one side to the other, adding prs and taking them out as required. Take occasional sewings into the 10-stick.

Braids

Lattice 3
Lotus 1

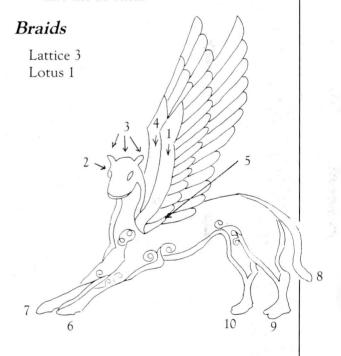

CHAPTER THREE

Colour

Using Colour

The use of colour in lacemaking is a subject of much debate. Some argue for, and some against, it. Both sides are convinced that they are right. What is indisputable, however, is that the real beauty of lace lies in its fine detail and in the intricate interweaving of the threads. Anything that detracts from this is taking away the essential element of the lace.

White thread is especially effective in lacemaking because it reflects light and casts shadows, which highlight the way the threads move. Can coloured threads do the same thing? This depends to a large extent on the kind of fabric the lacemaker is trying to create.

Milanese braids, as seen in this book and in its predecessor, *Milanese Lace*, are particularly adaptable for use with coloured thread, because they are worked with few pairs, and the patterns are assembled either in sections or in a meandering braid which can be sectionalized. Because there is no need to carry threads from one part of the work to another, as in Torchon, for instance, we can be more flexible and adventurous in the way we choose and combine colours.

The word 'colour' when applied to lace means more than simply variations in pigment. It can also be used to describe the relationship between one piece of fabric and another, between patterned and plain braid, and between one type of stitch and another. These relationships create both the constrasts between dense and open work, and the

illusion of light and shade. It is the lacemaker's personal conception of them, and the way in which he or she manipulates them, that give a piece of work its individual character.

When we plan a design in white Milanese lace, we are all concerned with colour/tone, without really being aware of it. Yet we manage to find perfectly acceptable combinations of dense and open fabrics, and to put together what 'looks' right. We are following that old adage: we know what we like, even if we don't know why we like it. When starting to think about colour as pigment, we must also continue to be concerned with colour in this wider sense.

Many of us worry about which colours to use when first making coloured lace. However, the choice can be just as instinctive as our choice of different braids. We do not live in a monochrome world: we are surrounded by colour all the time. As children we learn to speak because we hear others talking around us. Likewise, we learn about colour because we are surrounded by it and because we are constantly making decisions about it. For example, which shirt should we wear with which suit? Which flowers should we put together in a vase? Which curtains will complement the wallpaper, and which garnish should we add to a meal to make it look appetising? The list is endless, and do we ever stop to think about the theory of colour? Of course we don't.

Before using colour in a particular piece of lace we have a decision to make, which will affect our whole approach to the work. We have to decide whether the colour itself is to be our main concern, with the decorated parts of the braid an embellishment to the whole, or whether we are going to concentrate on the relationship between the braids, i.e. the balance between dense and open fabrics, and make the colour scheme of secondary importance. The difference is one of emphasis.

A third approach is to give equal prominence to the colour and the decorated braid. In this case, the lacemaker should first select a pattern and then plan the colour scheme by photocopying the pattern and colouring it in. Finally, the braids (which may be either patterned or plain) are chosen to match the colours.

Where the main aim is to blend colours together, plain cloth braids will usually create the best effect, permitting us to give our full attention to the colour, without the added complication of having to work a large number of different stitches. In other words, the colour should come first. This is not to say we should not include decorated braids, but that we should use them sparingly.

If, on the other hand, our purpose is to add some colour to the particular braids that have taken our fancy, we need to adopt a different set of criteria. The features of the braid must now be considered first, and the colour second. Thus the colour is fitted to the braid, and not the braid to the colour. Sometimes a colour will blur or even obliterate the pattern detail, and time taken to work an intricate braid will be wasted. Always work a sample of the braid in the colour you intend using. Lighter colours will cast shadows in a similar way to white thread, while darker colours will suit some braids but not all. If for some reason you particularly wish to use a certain colour and find it doesn't do justice to the braid, consider changing the braid for another.

The Three Approaches to Using Colour: A Summary

1 A colour scheme is planned first, and the braids are selected to fit this. Braids and colour are of equal importance in the design.

2 The choice of colour comes first and the braid stitches are an embellishment. With this approach, the way in which the colour is used is of prime importance.

3 Colour is used to enhance the braids, and is of secondary importance.

Whatever your approach, always bear in mind that the balance between plain and decorated braids, i.e. the relationship between dense and open fabric, is as important in coloured lace as it is in white. The difference is that the colour itself can sometimes alter this balance. Be alert to what is happening on the pillow, and be prepared to make adjustments.

Working with Colour: Some Practicalities

It saves a great deal of time and frustration to work out your ideas on paper before you even think about winding bobbins. Take several tracings or photocopies of your pattern and play around with colour ideas, both with and without particular braids. Next take several tracings or photocopies of actual braid diagrams and follow the passage of the threads with coloured pencils to discover what colour effects can be achieved with them. This method has the added bonus of teaching you a lot about the formation of the braids themselves. Remember that time spent experimenting can pay dividends.

Using Colour within a Pattern

1 Flat colour: use one colour per braid, keeping passives and weavers all the same colour.

2 Multi-coloured pattern: use several colours per braid. This effect may be achieved

   a by different-coloured passives

   b by different-coloured weavers

   c by interchanging threads, both passives and weavers, as the work progresses

3 Colours can also follow the passage of the threads within the braids themselves to create special effects.

4 A combination of any of the above.

Fiddling

When using colour, it is important to remember that fiddling is a legitimate technique. The natural run of the threads within a braid will not always take the colour where you want it to be, and you must therefore manipulate the threads.

Twist one thread around another (in addition to working the normal stitch) so that the path of the coloured thread is changed. Watch your tension at these points, and use a support pin if necessary.

Choosing Coloured Thread

Any coloured thread can be used. Adapt the scale of the pattern to the thread, just as you would if you were using white thread.

The Shepherdess: An Experiment

'The Shepherdess' is shown in colour between pp. 112 and 113, and in its white form with working instructions on pp. 69–72. It was worked by Lucy Kincaid as an experiment in the making of coloured lace.

A large piece of lace takes time to make and, as work progresses, colour ideas can change. The wrong colour left in place at an early stage can be disastrous. In this case, the lacemaker's first priority was to create balanced 'white' lace. The work had to stand on its own merit as lace, with the colour an optional extra.

When the work reached the point where it would, under normal circumstances, have been thought finished, the lace was unpinned and placed on a polystyrene block. With paintbrush and fabric dyes (and heart in mouth!) colour was applied to the finished lace. A step was being taken into the unknown, and anything could have happened. But it is only by experimenting that we can make discoveries, and sometimes it is worth taking a risk in order to add a new technique to our repertoire.

If at the end of your foray into making coloured lace you decide that it isn't for you, and that you really prefer white lace, then your conclusion will have been reached from practical, 'hands-on' experience and your argument will have validity. However, you will also have expanded your knowledge of lacemaking techniques.

Left: *Dragon* (p. 113)

Below: *Butterfly* (p. 114)

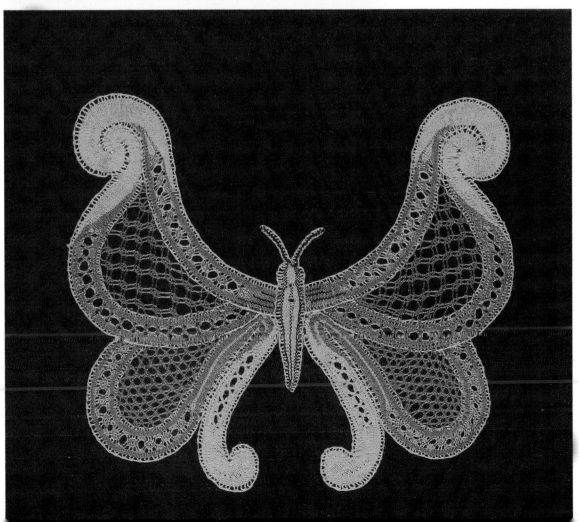

Fan (pp. 116-17)

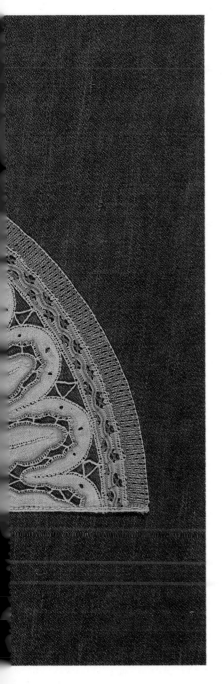

Kingfisher (p. 115)

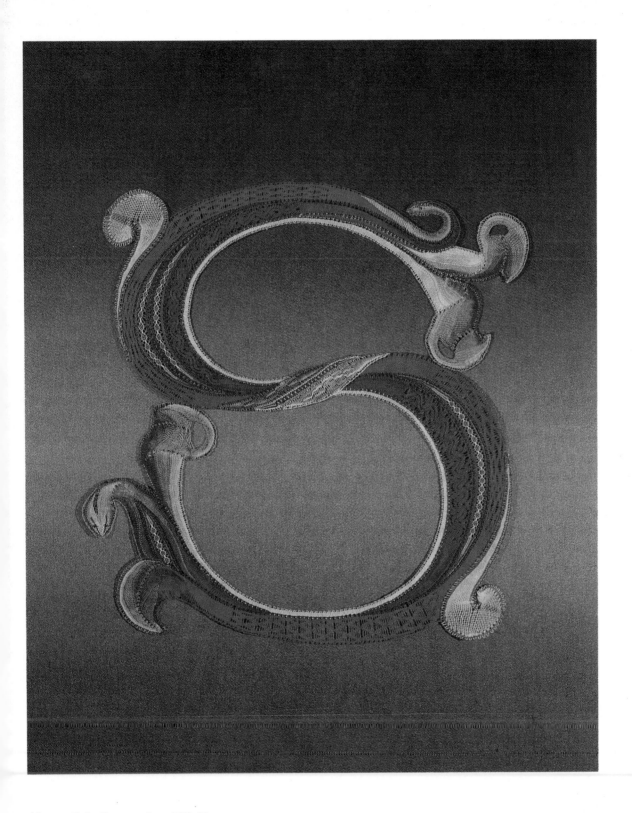

Above: *S for Serpent (pp. 120-2)*

Left: *Garland (pp. 118-19)*

Left: *Medieval Peacock (pp. 123-24)*

Below: *Shell Fan (pp. 125-9)*

Overleaf: *The Shepherdess (pp. 69-73)*

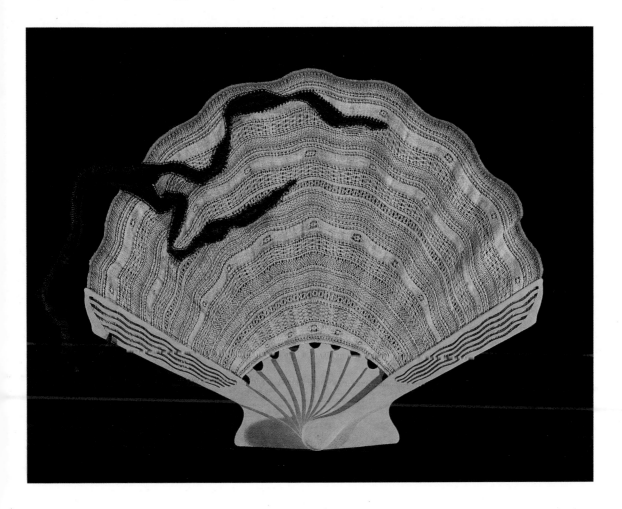

Dragon

Designed and worked by Patricia Read. See Colour plate between pp. 112 and 113.

Thread

DMC Brilliante d'Alsace 50
Yellow 307, Green 3346, Red 666
Madeira metallic gold (for feet)

Order of Working

1 Nose and head work through continuously to point at tail.

2 Lower jaw.

3 Start crest at outer tip. When sewing off into top of head, turn 3 prs to work the narrow braid on the outside, adding 2 prs more as work progresses.

4 Tongue and flame.

5 Ten-stick on crest, beard and tail.*

6 Claws

* Lacemakers with experience of Honiton techniques may prefer to work these as the braid is made. Detailed instructions are given on p. 143 ('Leaf with Raised Veins') of *The Technique of Honiton Lace* by Elsie Luxton (Batsford).

Braid

Hooked 2

Butterfly

Designed by Jane and worked by Patricia Read. See colour plate between pp. 112 and 113.

Thread

DMC Brilliante d'Alsace 50 in five shades

Order of Working

1   Antennae and body.

2   Upper wings, starting by sewing prs into body.

3   Lower wings, starting with scroll.

4   Fillings

Ws and edge prs are in a neutral shade of grey except for the scrolls on the lower wings and the scroll method on the curved tips of the upper wings, where a denser colour was achieved by using the same colour Ws as the passives.

Braids

> Daisy 2
> Roundel 2

Fillings

> Hooked 2
> Mesh 1

Kingfisher

An original design worked by Pauline Beard.
See colour plate between pp. 112 and 113.

Threads

The original was worked in the following:
Madeira Rayon 40: Orange 1065
Madeira Mettalic 40: Turquoise 9842
DMC Broder Machine 50: Peacock Green
943, Electric Blue 806, Black 310, and White.

You may prefer to use threads and colours of
your own choice. Adjust the scale of the
pattern to fit the thickness of the thread.

Order of Working

1   Head: blue, orange and white sections in
    that order.

2   Lower face: blue section first, then white.

3   Beak: upper
    then lower.

4   Main blue feather along back.

5   Second blue feather along back.

6   Blue wing. Starting at front edge work
    towards flight feathers. Start each feather
    at the tip and finish by sewing off.

7   Orange wing. Small feathers first, then
    the larger ones. Start each feather at the
    tip and sew off to finish. Work away
    from body.

8   Body.

9   Tail.

10 Attach beads for the eye.

Braids

Lattice 1
Half-stitch (for body)

Fan

Designed and worked by Patricia Read. See colour plate between pp. 112 and 113.

Thread

DMC Brilliante d'Alsace 50 in cream, plus two shades each of pink and green.

Order of Working

The braids are in long sections. Therefore the pattern should be on one piece of card only. For ease of working, use a mushroom pillow not less than 45cm. (18in.) in diameter.

1 Use 6 prs for the 10-stick along the bottom edge of one side, keeping the *edge stitch on the pattern side* and the *turning stitch on the outside*. There are 2 reasons for this: the ts gives a smooth and neat edge to the work, while the pin holes of the edge st are on the inside, nearest to where sewings will be taken from the other braids. When the 10-stick reaches the lower braid, hang more prs and turn the pillow.

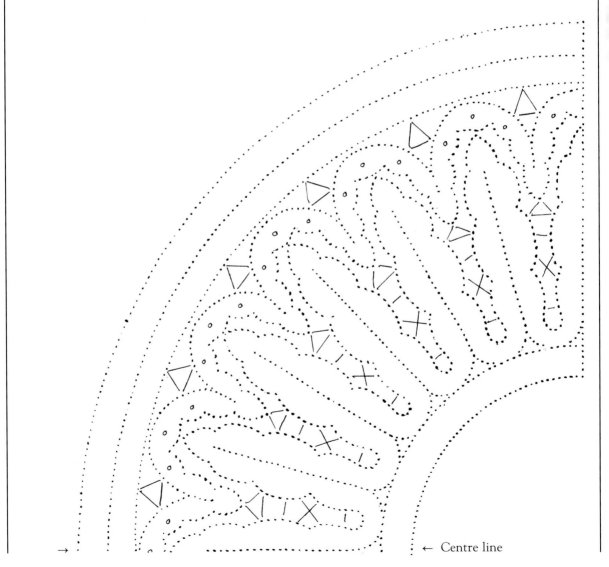

← Centre line

2   Work the lower braid to the other side of the fan. When the last hole is reached, turn the pillow and work 10-stick with 6 prs to the outer edge. As the last few holes are worked, reduce to 4 prs. These can be tied back and cut.

3   The individual sections of the fan. Make the joining bars as work progresses.

4   The arches over the sections. Again, make the joining bars as work progresses.

5   The inner of the two outside braids.

6   The outer braid.

Braids

Lattice 3	Holes (p. 43)
Cross-bud	Meander with Rose

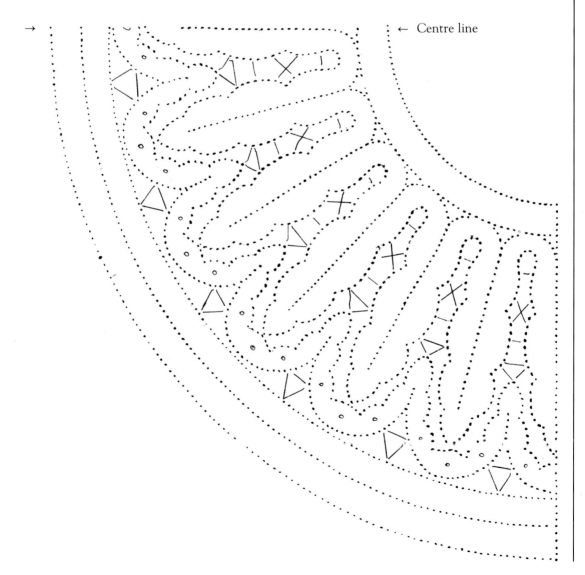

← Centre line

Garland

Designed and worked by Sandi Woods. See colour plate between pp. 112 and 113.

Threads

The choice and number of colours used are entirely at the lacemaker's discretion. The original was worked in DMC Special Dentelles 80 (cotton), nos 223, 677, 3013, 926, 315, 437, 3345 and 823.

To Work

The pricking represents half of the finished piece. The three sections can be rearranged if desired, or used individually.

Keep plenty of bobbins to hand, wound with small amounts of thread. When a colour is no longer needed, tie and throw back in the normal way. *Do not* cut off a colour until you are quite sure you are finished with it.

The numbers on the pattern indicate the order in which the braids should be worked.

Braids

Daisy 2
Lattice 3 (used as a filling)

S for Serpent

Winner of the Batsford Prize (First Place) 1993

Designed and worked by Sandi Woods. See colour plate between pp. 112 and 113.

Threads

The choice and number of colours used are entirely at the lacemaker's discretion. If necessary, adjust the size of the pattern to the thickness of the thread. The original was worked in Gutermann Silk S303, nos 3, 483, 893, 218, 214, 582, 870, 416, 309, 482, 703, 841, 810 and 585.

To Work

Keep plenty of bobbins to hand, wound with small amounts of thread. When a colour is no longer required, tie and throw back in the normal way. *Do not* cut off a colour until you are sure you no longer need it.

The numbers on the pattern indicate the order in which the braids should be worked. Finish by attaching beads for the eyes.

Braids

Lotus 2
Running River
Cross-net

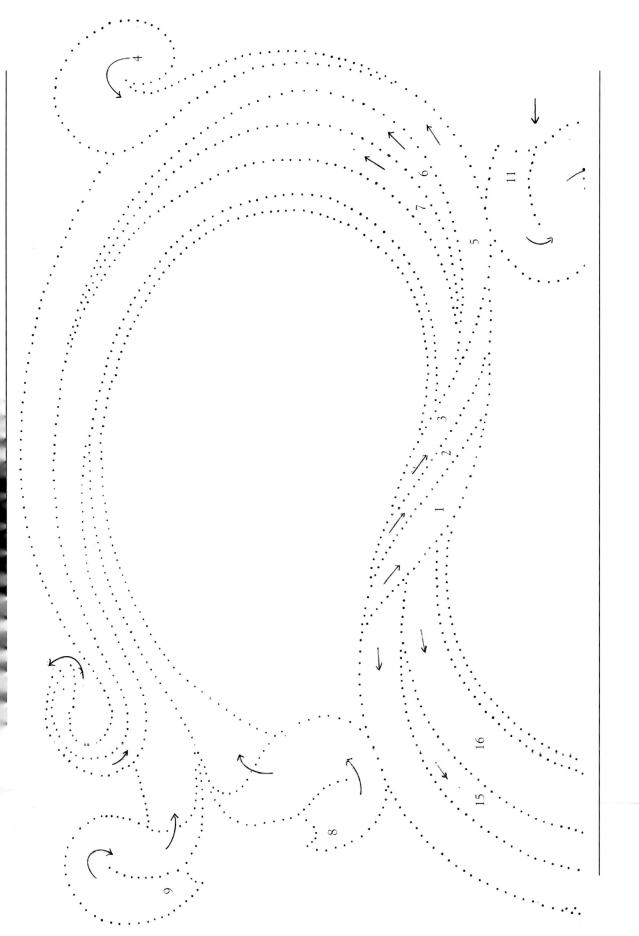

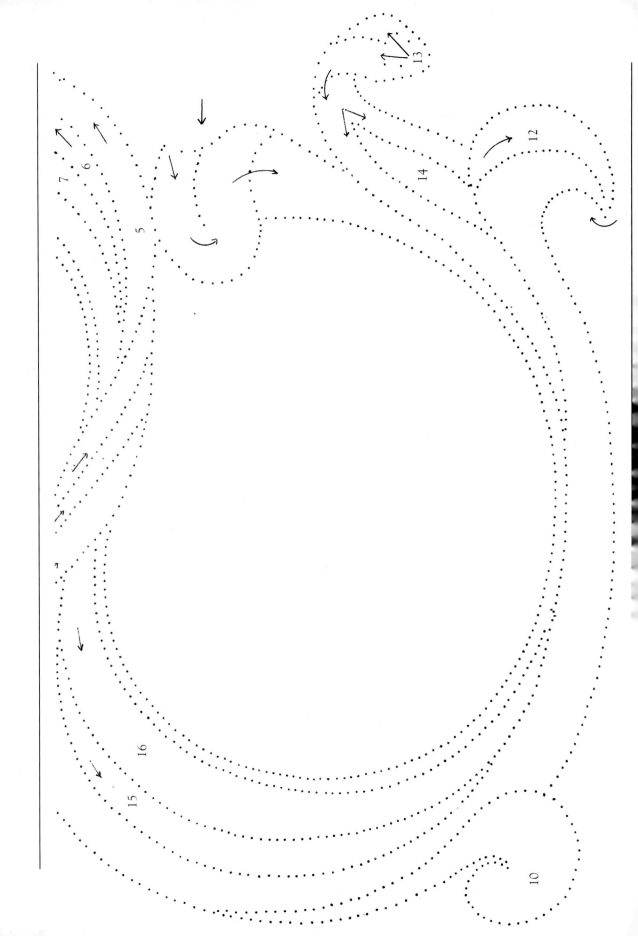

Medieval Peacock

Designed and worked by Sandi Woods. See colour plate between pp. 112 and 113.

Threads

The choice and number of colours are entirely at the lacemaker's discretion. If necessary, adjust the size of the pattern to the thickness of the thread. The original was worked in Gutermann Silk S303, nos 412, 841, 482, 703, 582, 309, 483, 402, 585, 214 and 870.

To Work

Keep plenty of bobbins to hand, wound with small amounts of thread. When a colour is no longer required, tie and throw back in the normal way. *Do not* cut off a colour until you are sure you no longer need it.

The numbers on the pattern indicate the order in which the braids should be worked. Finish by attaching beads for the eyes.

Braids

Bubbles
Roundel 2
Open Spider
Lattice 1

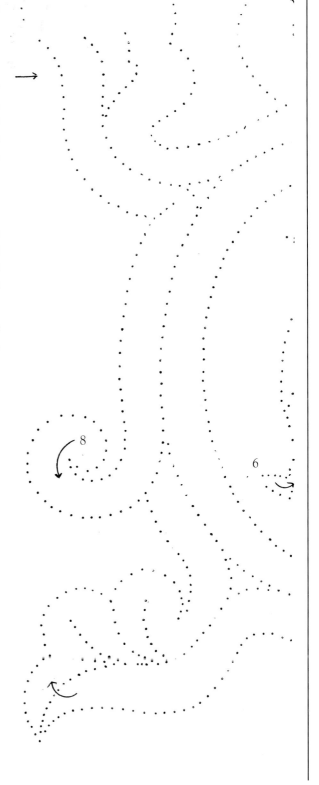

Shell Fan

Winner of the Nancy Armstrong Lace Fan Award and the Ian Ferris Trophy 1993

Designed and worked by Sandi Woods. See colour plate between pp. 112 and 113.

Threads

The choice of thread and colours is at the lacemaker's discretion. If necessary, adjust the size of the pattern to the thickness of the thread. The original was worked in Gutermann Silk S303, nos 3, 5, 37, 43, 50, 130, 143, 158, 213, 215, 369, 472, 568, 585, 658, 659, 707, 800, 802, 841 and 893.

To Work

A scallop shell was the inspiration for this project. The natural lines and markings on the shell readily lend themselves to the use of decorated braids. The seaweed has been added to give a three-dimensional, *trompe-l'œil* effect and is mostly worked within the shape of the shell. However, a small piece is worked outside the line of the pattern and flipped over when the work is removed from the pillow. To emphasize the three-dimensional appearance, shading has been worked under parts of the seaweed, by introducing darker thread into the braids. Where shading is required, lines should be drawn onto the pricking before work commences, to serve as a reminder.

Keep plenty of bobbins to hand, wound with small amounts of thread. When a colour is no longer required, tie and throw back in the normal way. *Do not* cut off a colour until you are sure you no longer need it.

The arrows on the pricking denote fold lines and the sticks are centred between them. Side sewings are used for sewing off the lower section of seaweed into the upper part, and also for sewing in pairs to start each braid up the side of the fan. Use side sewings, too, when sewing out each pair on the other side. Top sewings, which give a slightly raised or ridged effect on the right side of the work, have been used for joining each strip of braid.

The braids used to make the original fan are listed below, but these may be substituted by other braids in this book. Working diagrams for Ovals, Pinwheel and Ribbon are given on pp. 44–5. These are also illustrated with detailed instructions in our previous book *Milanese Lace*. The narrowest bands of braid in this pattern are worked in cloth stitch.

The fan should be worked in the following order:

Seaweed

Work in cloth stitch throughout. Start at the outside point, continue through the upper section and tie back at the point. Start at the point of the lower section and sew off into the upper section.

Outlining

Work in 10-stick using 7 pairs. It is important to note that this 10-stick is made with the turning stitch on the *outside* of the work, which gives a smooth appearance to the edge of the fan. This means that the edge stitch is on the inside, and as there will be many sewings into it 3 twists should be given to the edge pair and the workers. Make the 10-stick very carefully, taking great care with the tension.

Pairs for the 10-stick are sewn into the top section of seaweed, worked round the top of the fan, down the side, round the short base (still with the turning stitch on the outside of the work), up the side and along the remainder of the top, before being sewn off into the seaweed.

Lines of Braid

Each braid is worked in turn, starting with the shortest at the bottom of the fan. Pairs for the braids should be sewn into the 10-stick on the seaweed side and sewn off on the opposite side, using side sewings. Each braid will have an edge stitch on one side only. Thus there will be no edge stitch on the side of the adjoining braid where top sewings are to be made. Nor will there be an edge stitch on either side of the final braid at the top of the fan, where the work is joined with top sewings into the adjacent braid and with side sewings into the 10-stick.

Braids

Fish 2
Lattice
Ovals
Pinwheel
Ribbon
Maltese Spot*

*   *Note* Where it was felt necessary to make the Maltese Spot more elongated, the workers have been crossed 2 or 3 times in the centre instead of once as in the diagram on p. 43.

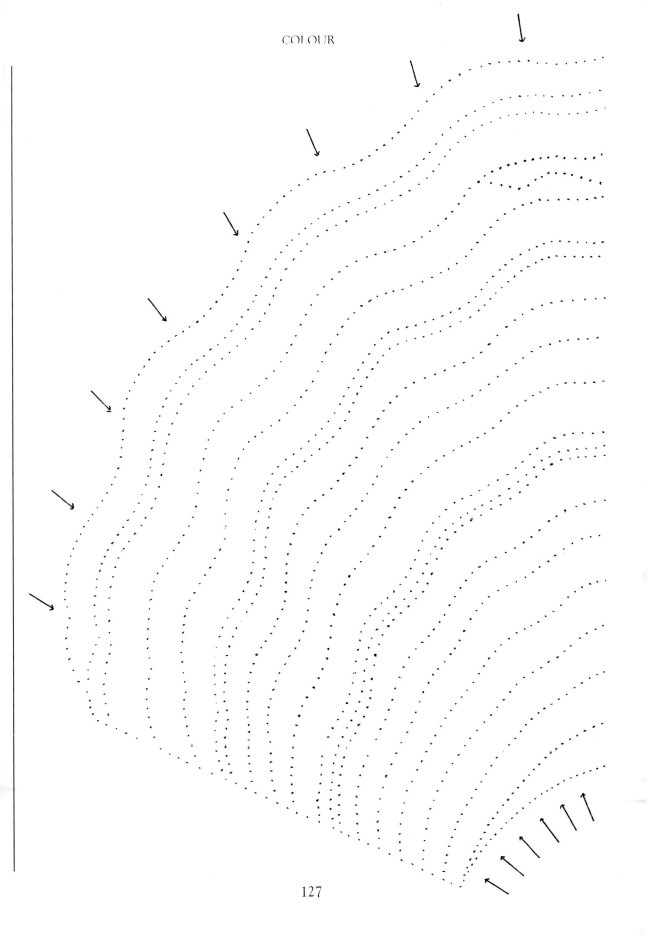

128

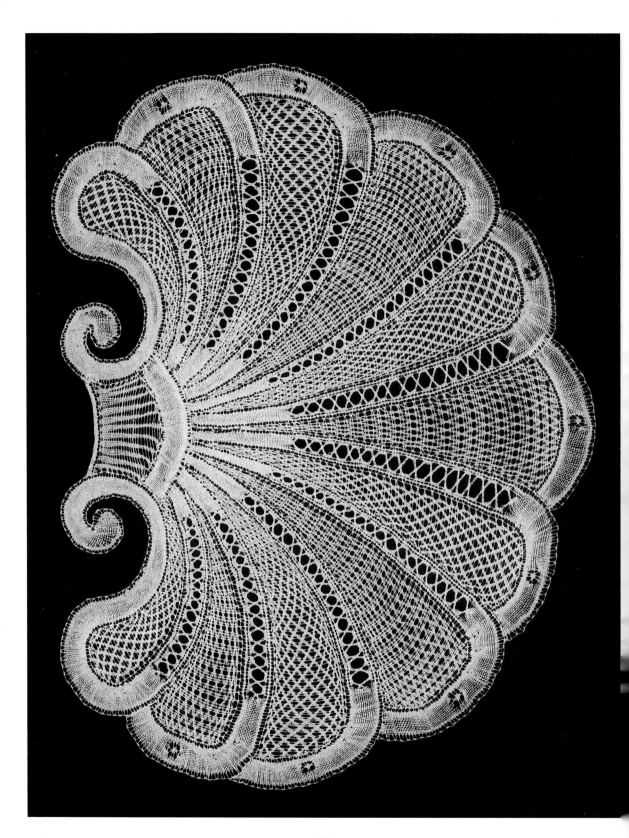

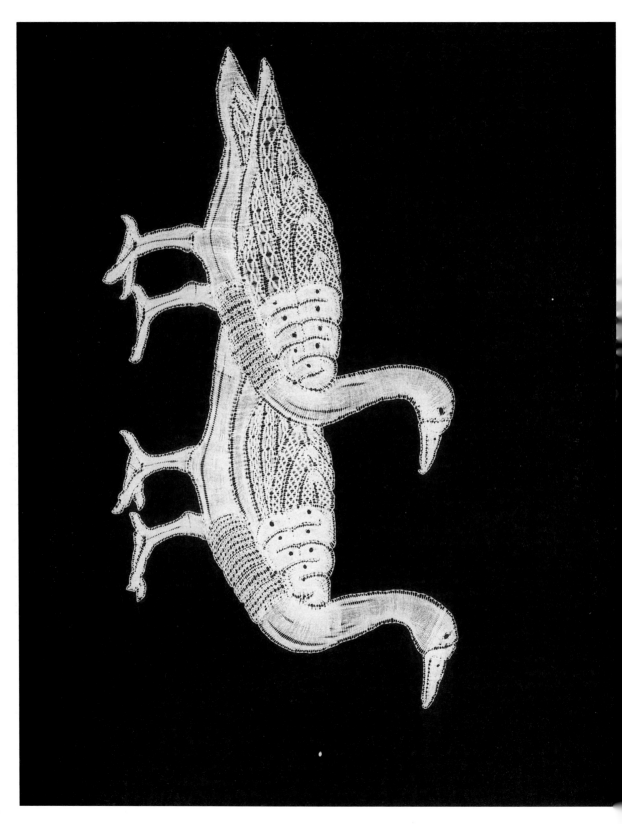

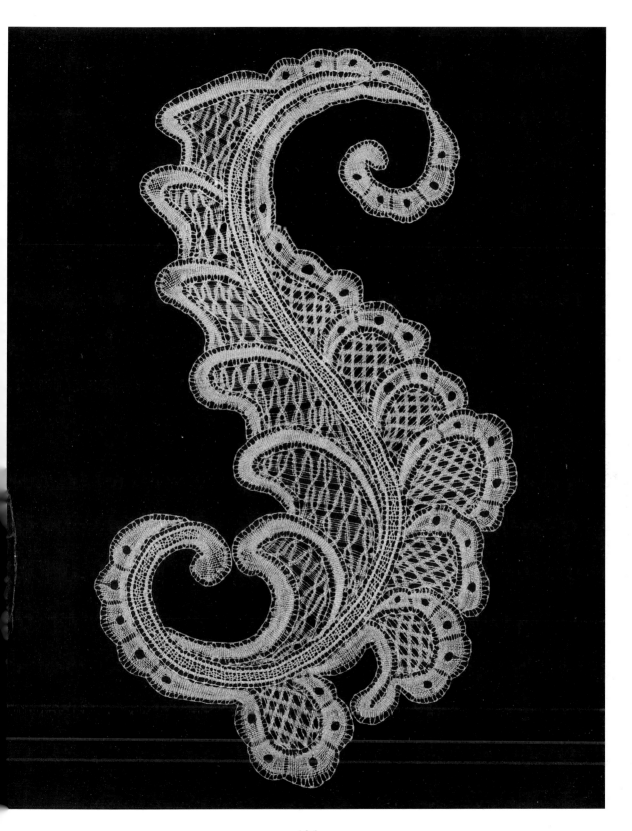

Index